Battle Orders • 26

US Airborne Units in the Pacific Theater 1942–45

Gordon L Rottman

Consultant Editor Dr Duncan Anderson • *Series editors* Marcus Cowper and Nikolai Bogdanovic

First published in Great Britain in 2007 by Osprey Publishing,
Midland House, West Way, Botley, Oxford OX2 0PH, UK
443 Park Avenue South, New York, NY 10016, USA
E-mail: info@ospreypublishing.com

ISBN 978 184603 128 1

Editorial by Ilios Publishing Ltd (www.iliospublishing.com)
Page layout by Bounford.com, Huntingdon. UK
Index by Alison Worthington
Typeset in GillSans and Stone Serif
Originated by United Graphics, Singapore
Printed in China through Bookbuilders

07 08 09 10 11   10 9 8 7 6 5 4 3 2 1

A CIP catalog record for this book is available from the British Library.

For a catalog of all books published by Osprey Military and Aviation please contact:
Osprey Direct USA, c/o Random House Distribution Center, 400 Hahn Rd,
Westminster, MD 21157 USA
E-mail: info@ospreydirect.com
Osprey Direct UK, P.O. Box 140, Wellingborough, Northants, NN8 2FA, UK
E-mail: info@ospreydirect.co.uk
www.ospreypublishing.com

Image credits

The photographic images that appear in this work were obtained
from the National Archives and Records Administration.

Author's note

The author is indebted to Edward M. Flanagain, Jr. (Lt Gen, Rtd),
Stuart Kohn, and Yves J. Bellanger for their assistance.
Following the styles used by different nations, in the unit
designations in this book US units are labeled, for example,
503d Parachute Infantry Regiment, whereas Commonwealth
units are labeled, for example, 2nd Parachute Brigade Group.

In the tree diagrams and maps in this volume, the units and
movements of national forces are depicted in the following colors:

US Army units	Blue
US Marine Corps units	Olive Drab
Japanese units	Red
Australian units	Brown

For a key to the symbols used in this volume, see below.

When multiple unit commanders are listed for a unit, the date of
the first commander is the date the unit commenced participation
in the operation and not the date he assumed command. Officers
shown as wounded in action (WIA), but not followed by a
replacing officer were returned to duty.

Measurements and weapon calibers

Distances, ranges, and dimensions are mostly given in the
contemporary US system of inches, feet, yards, and statute miles.
A simple conversion table is provided below.

feet to meters	multiply feet by 0.3048
yards to meters	multiply yards by 0.9114
miles to kilometers	multiply miles by 1.6093
centimeters to inches	multiply centimeters by 0.3937

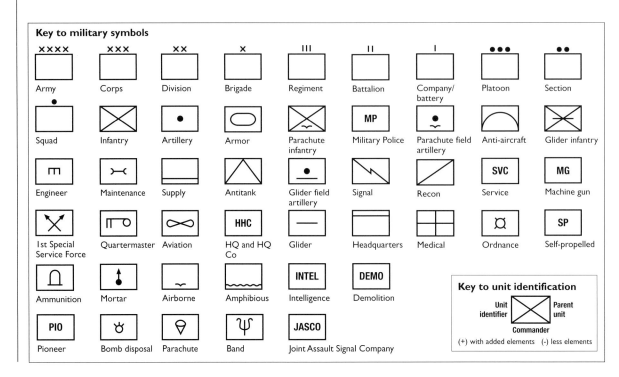

Contents

Introduction

The Pacific Theater of Operations (PTO) is often forgotten in the study of World War II airborne operations. The reasons are several: the operations there were much smaller in scale and generally had less decisive effects than in other theaters. Only a single airborne division, the 11th, was deployed to the PTO, and it conducted only a single regimental parachute operation and no significant glider assaults; most of its combat deployment was as ground troops delivered by sea. The other Army parachute unit in theater was the 503d Parachute Infantry Regiment (PIR), which conducted three regimental operations; it too had its share of ground combat. The four United States Marine Corps (USMC) parachute battalions conducted no parachute operations, but proved their value in amphibious and ground economy-of-force operations. Counting both Army and Marine airborne units, there were only nine parachute and four glider battalions deployed to the PTO, plus the three 1st Special Service Force (FSSF) battalion-sized regiments.

Although two operations in particular – the Corregidor assault and the Los Baños raid – were among the most spectacular and successful airborne operations of World War II, some have questioned the value of the contribution of airborne forces in the PTO fighting. While certain operations could have been accomplished without airborne unit participation, the forces did contribute to their success, even if their involvement did not prove decisive or if the operation did not go entirely to plan. Their ability to move rapidly by air provided a useful capability, and their light equipment and logistics tail made them useful over the theater's rugged terrain. The inherent flexibility of airborne units, gained through their training and philosophy, allowed them to respond rapidly to emerging situations and economy-of-force missions.

The 2d InfDiv was provided air transport training prior to the war and many of the developments were later adapted by the airborne. The Douglas C-32 (derived from the DC-2), predecessor of the C-47, was used for this task. (National Museum of the US Air Force)

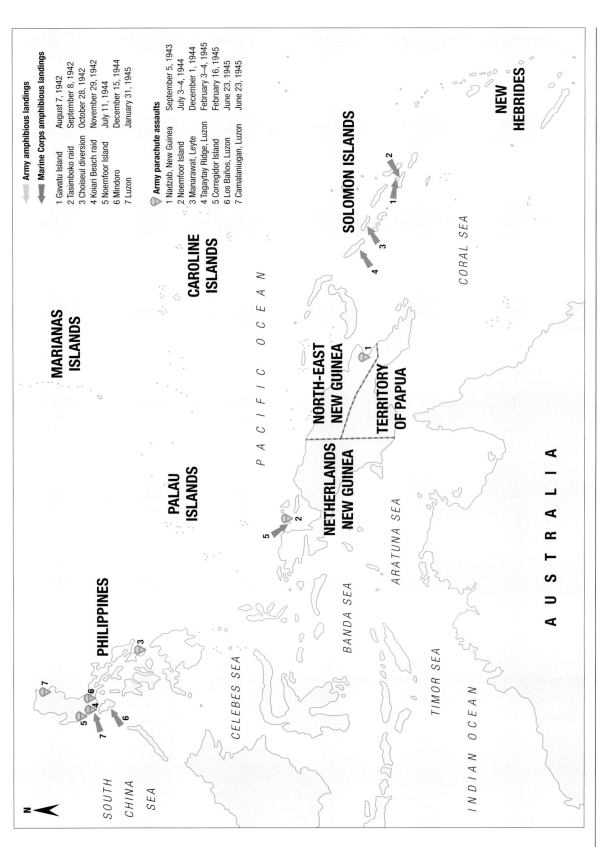

Army amphibious landings

Marine Corps amphibious landings

1 Gavatu Island — August 7, 1942
2 Tasimboko raid — September 8, 1942
3 Choiseul diversion — October 28, 1942
4 Koiari Beach raid — November 29, 1942
5 Noemfoor Island — July 11, 1944
6 Mindoro — December 15, 1944
7 Luzon — January 31, 1945

Army parachute assaults

1 Nadzab, New Guinea — September 5, 1943
2 Noemfoor Island — July 3–4, 1944
3 Manarawat, Leyte — December 1, 1944
4 Tagaytay Ridge, Luzon — February 3–4, 1945
5 Corregidor Island — February 16, 1945
6 Los Baños, Luzon — June 23, 1945
7 Camalaniugan, Luzon — June 23, 1945

MARIANAS ISLANDS

CAROLINE ISLANDS

PALAU ISLANDS

PHILIPPINES

NEW HEBRIDES

SOLOMON ISLANDS

NORTH-EAST NEW GUINEA

NETHERLANDS NEW GUINEA

TERRITORY OF PAPUA

AUSTRALIA

PACIFIC OCEAN

CORAL SEA

ARATUNA SEA

BANDA SEA

CELEBES SEA

TIMOR SEA

INDIAN OCEAN

SOUTH CHINA SEA

N

The Southwest Pacific. US airborne operations are indicated together with amphibious landings conducted by airborne units.

Combat mission

The US Army issued guidelines for airborne missions in May 1942, before conducting any exercises larger than at battalion level; it already envisaged larger operations than this. The guidelines were very much based on an analysis of the successful, though costly, German operations of 1940–41.

Parachute units were capable of seizing and holding terrain suitable for the landing of troop-carrying airplanes and gliders, river and canal crossings and defiles, areas to the rear of enemy beach defenses, and landing fields for the operation of friendly aircraft or to deny their use to the enemy. They could also establish bridgeheads, attack defended positions in the rear or flank, land within and attack the interior of a perimeter defense, seize or destroy enemy supply and communication installations, assist ground offensives by vertical envelopment and seizure of terrain and enemy establishments, and operate in conjunction with armored forces by consolidating and holding gains, creating confusion, and conducting diversions.

In all theaters, many parachute operations were in support of an amphibious assault or ground offensive, aiming to either secure objectives inland and await a link up with the amphibious force, block enemy advances toward the beachhead, and create confusion, or reinforce an established beachhead. The parachute delivery of reinforcements allowed the rapid introduction of significant numbers of troops without having to wait for a return trip by the initial landing craft to the port of embarkation; this in turn allowed the previous landing craft to be used for other missions, and prevented their exposure to enemy air and sea attack when returning to the beachhead.

Airborne units generally conducted larger operations in the European and Mediterranean theaters than in the Pacific. The single-division southern France, three-division (two US and one British) Normandy and Netherlands, and two-division Rhine crossing operations were vastly larger and more complex than any conducted in the PTO. Such operations would not be conducted in the Pacific owing to terrain restrictions, airlift limitations, rapidly changing situations, and the nature of the enemy. It is surprising how often airborne operations in the Mediterranean and Europe were in support of amphibious operations, while in the Pacific – an amphibious warfare environment – they were seldom so.

Only seven combat parachute operations, of regimental or smaller size, were conducted in the PTO. Two missions blocked enemy withdrawal routes, one of which also had the objective of capturing an airstrip. Another mission served to secure a dominating terrain feature and a friendly avenue of advance. It also provided rapid aerial reinforcement of amphibious troops. Only one mission had the goal of seizing an island, and was supported by a small amphibious landing. One mission reinforced an amphibious assault on an island, and another small mission, actually conducted over several days, served to position an artillery battery in an advantageous position and provide reinforcement. A more spectacular mission was a parachute-delivered raid to liberate civilian internees.

While there were glider units in the PTO, no significant glider operations were conducted. There were, however, several operations in which airborne units, both parachute and glider, fought as ground troops or conducted economy-of-force missions after being delivered by sea.

Doctrine called for airborne units to be withdrawn from combat after three to four days under ideal conditions, or if necessary within 30 days. This allowed the unit to return to base, rebuild, and train for its next operation. To tie airborne

This photograph was taken on Leyte, but it could have been on any of the islands on which airborne troops fought in the Pacific. The terrain and climate were almost as much of a challenge as the resolute enemy.

A battalion 81mm mortar section set up on Mount Malepunyo, southern Luzon. Mortars were extremely valuable to airborne troops. They could be man-packed forward and so long as there was a small clearing or opening in the trees they could provide responsive fire support. On Choiseul Marine paratroopers, unable to find clearings, set up their 60mm mortars in the beach waters, with only the muzzle above water, to fire on a Japanese supply dump.

units down in prolonged battles after their initial mission was accomplished was to waste a valuable asset. Tactical necessity sometimes required an airborne unit to remain in combat for longer, especially if there were insufficient units to relieve them or if there were no pending operations in which they might be used. However, prolonged combat would mean higher casualties and greater fatigue, and there might be insufficient time to rebuild, train replacements, and plan and rehearse its next operation, which might arise unforeseen. Parachute-qualified replacements were also scarce, did not always arrive on a timely basis, and took time to become integrated into a unit. Provided below is a breakdown of the number of days spent in combat for parachute-inserted units in the PTO. The Leyte operation, which was an amphibious landing and did not involve an airborne operation, saw the units in action for 28 days. The Marine 1st Parachute Battalion, although not parachute delivered, spent 54 days in action on Guadalcanal and 34 days on Bougainville.

Operation	Unit	Days in action
Nadzab, New Guinea	503d PIR	14
Noemfoor Island	503d PIR	60
Luzon	511th PIR	90
Corregidor	503d PIR	21
Camalaniugan	1/511th PIR	11

Marine Corps parachute units[1] were intended to support the primary mission of the Fleet Marine Force (FMF), which was to secure advanced navy bases in support of a naval campaign. It was envisioned that they would parachute onto enemy-held islands and seize inland objectives in advance of an amphibious assault force. Objectives could include airfields, bridges, road intersections, key terrain, and areas that would facilitate the amphibious force's advance inland. Secondary missions were small-scale raids and reconnaissance missions, both parachute- and boat-delivered; in reality, these would become their primary missions. Their normal method of operation was in support of a division seizing an island lodgment, and seldom operated in larger than battalion size.

---

1 Marine parachute units are popularly called "Paramarines," although the USMC dislikes this term as it implies they are "half-Marines."

Unit status

The battle blaze of the 1st Marine Parachute Regiment. Prior to the formation of the regiment the parachute battalions did not wear a sleeve insignia. This was a modified I Marine Amphibious Corps insignia.

Marine parachute units

The Marine Corps initiated its airborne effort in October 1940 when 40 trainees began parachute and rigger training at Lakehurst, NJ – the Navy's Aircrew Survival Equipmentman School.[2] Additional classes were graduated through the summer of 1941, and it was realized that the training facilities were inadequate for the numbers of jumpers needed; alternating classes were sent to the East and West Coast parachute battalions. There were also problems obtaining enough volunteers, due to the competition for troops among the growing divisions. It was not until May and June 1942 that parachute training schools were established at San Diego, CA and New River, NC respectively. The first two of four parachute battalions were activated in July 1941, although at the time there were not enough transports available to drop even a company. In August 1941 a company was parachuted into an East Coast landing exercise, demonstrating the confusion they could cause to an enemy force.

The Marine requirement for parachute units was, like the Army's, largely influenced by German successes. In view of the German use of airborne troops to seize objectives in advance of ground forces, the Corps felt they could be employed the same way in advance of amphibious forces. The Marines were aware they fielded only a relatively small combat force, and were more than willing to examine any new idea that might multiply their combat power and be of use to their primary mission as a land force in support of a naval campaign.

The Marine Corps' formation of parachute units began modestly with the activation of 1st Platoon, 2d Parachute Company on March 10, 1941 at San Diego, CA. At the time it was planned to assign only a single company per division. This was part of a proposal for one infantry battalion per regiment to be trained as "air infantry," and for one of the battalion's companies to be parachute trained. This concept, of course, would not have worked, as the battalion was expected to perform similar missions to the other battalions in the regiment. The time available to conduct specialized training would have been limited and when needed for air-delivered missions it might already be engaged in other missions. A May 1940 concept for a deployed parachute battalion included a two-gun platoon of 75mm pack howitzers, attached antitank and antiaircraft guns as necessary, no vehicles other then hand carts, three units of fire for all weapons, and three days' rations and water. An August 1941 proposal was for an "air attack brigade" with a parachute and an air infantry regiment for each of the Marine divisions.

1st Platoon, 2d Parachute Company became Company A, 2d Parachute Battalion on May 1, 1941. Company A, 1st Parachute Battalion was activated on May 28 at Quantico, VA. Company A, 2d Parachute Battalion was attached to the 1st Provisional Marine Brigade en route to Iceland, but did not accompany it. Instead it was redesignated Company B, 1st Parachute Battalion on September 20. The 1st Parachute Battalion was activated at Quantico on August 15 followed by the 2d on October 1 at Quantico. The Parachute School was slow to produce jumpers to fill the battalions. The 3d Parachute Battalion was activated at San Diego on September 16, 1942.

These battalions were originally assigned to the 1st–3d Marine Divisions (MarDivs), but were formally transferred to I Marine Amphibious Corps (IMAC)

---

2 For details of the genesis of Army airborne units, see Battle Orders 22: *US Airborne Units in the Mediterranean Theater 1942–44*, pp. 8–9.

Formation of the 1st Marine Parachute Battalion, 1941

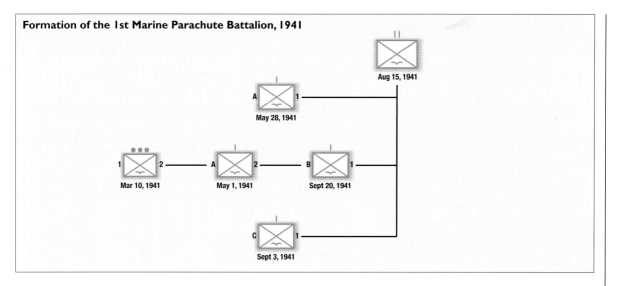

in January 1943. Only the 1st Battalion actually served with its parent division. The 1st Battalion moved from Quantico to New River, NC for training on September 28, 1941. Its Company C was activated on March 28, 1942. 2d Battalion's Company B was activated on July 23, 1941 at San Diego, CA and the battalion on October 1 followed by a new Company A on February 7, 1942 and Company C on September 3.

The 1st Battalion departed New River on June 7, 1942 and on the 10th shipped out of Norfolk, VA for the Pacific. Arriving at Wellington, New Zealand on July 11, it joined with the 1st MarDiv. A week later it sailed with the division first to Fiji for rehearsals and then to Guadalcanal, where it was to be the first US parachute unit to see action.

The 2d Battalion sailed from San Diego, CA on October 20, 1942 and arrived in Wellington on the 31st, where it remained until January 6, 1943 when it sailed to New Caledonia. In the meantime the 3d Parachute Battalion was activated with Company A on September 16, 1942 at San Diego, CA. Companies B and C were activated on November 10 and December 10, respectively. It departed in two echelons on March 5 and 13, 1943 to arrive at New Caledonia on the 27th.

There the three battalions were assembled at Camp Kiser outside of Tonotouta and formed into the IMAC Parachute Group, a training and administrative organization. IMAC understood by now that parachute operations in the South Pacific were impractical owing to the tactical environment, terrain, and lack of aircraft. Training was reoriented toward economy-of-force, reconnaissance, and amphibious operations. For all practical purposes the paratroopers were performing the same missions as the Marine Raiders. The Marines started having second thoughts as to the value of parachute units as early as the fall of 1942. No aircraft were available for jump training in the PTO after May 1943.

On April 1, 1943 the 1st Parachute Regiment was activated on New Caledonia for tactical control of all parachute battalions. At the same time the parachute battalions were formally removed from the divisions. A parachute school was briefly operated by the regiment for volunteers from local Marine units. The regiment deployed to Villa Lavella in early October 1943. Regimental units saw action on Choiseul and Bougainville, their final engagements.

The 2d Battalion was sent to Guadalcanal, while the rest of the regiment was on Bougainville. Following the decision to disband the parachute units, they departed for San Diego, CA in January 1944. The West Coast Parachute School was closed at the same time.

The East Coast Parachute Training Battalion had been closed on July 1, 1943. Its cadre and students were organized into the 4th Parachute Battalion on the same date. The 4th Battalion moved to San Diego, CA and was deactivated on January 19 without ever having served with the regiment. The rest of the regiment was deactivated on February 29. The 5th MarDiv was meanwhile being organized, and paratrooper enlisted men were reassigned, with 1st Battalion veterans going to the 26th Marines, 2d Battalion veterans to the 27th Marines, 3d Battalion veterans to the 28th Marines, and the 4th Battalion troops split between the three regiments[3] – some 3,000 men. The officers were assigned throughout the division as needed. The regiment's Air Delivery Section was split to provide the IMAC (redesignated IIIAC April 15, 1944) and VAC Air Delivery Sections. In August 1945 they reorganized as the 1st and 2d Air Delivery Platoons with 82 men apiece.

The 1940 concept of an "air infantry" battalion in each infantry regiment envisioned that they would be delivered by glider. No "air troop" units were organized, but a fledging glider unit was. The Marines had to rely on the Navy's Bureau of Aeronautics for gliders and it was none too enthused with the concept. The Marines desired a 12-place glider that could take off and land on water, carry a jeep or 37mm antitank gun, allow paratroopers to jump from it, and mount self-defense machine guns. Seventy-five would be required to transport a single air infantry battalion. Two such 900-man battalions were now envisioned rather than one in each of the six infantry regiments. A considerable problem was that even under double-tow, it would require two utility squadrons to tow one battalion's gliders. The Marines had only two under-equipped squadrons in 1941 and they were in constant demand for innumerable tasks.

The Glider Detachment was formed at Cherry Point, NC on January 10, 1942 to test equipment and provide glider training, which was initially undertaken at private schools. One- and two-man training gliders were not available until mid 1942. Showing some promise, Glider Group 71 (MLG-71) with Headquarters and Service Squadron 71 and Glider Squadron 711 (VML-711) were activated on April 24, 1942 at Parris Island, with 238 authorized personnel. A new training site was selected at Eagle Mountain Lake, TX and the unit moved there on November 24. Combat operations in the South Pacific demonstrated there were few opportunities to employ gliders, even if sufficient tug aircraft were available. The glider program was cancelled on June 24, 1943. The ten completed, 12-place, LRW-1 gliders were delivered to the Army, which never used them.

11th Airborne Division

The 11th AbnDiv was activated on February 25, 1943 at Camp Mackall as an Army of the United States formation (i.e. comprising regular cadres and conscripted troops), under the command of Maj Gen Joseph M. Swing. The cadre had been assembling for a few weeks, with most of the officers provided by the 76th InfDiv and the enlisted men from the 88th InfDiv. More officers and enlisted men came from Airborne Command units. Fillers began arriving on March 2 and thousands more continued to arrive from all over the country for weeks. Few had undergone basic training at a replacement training center, and would undertake this within the division. Most were 18–20 years old and more than 60 percent had an Army General Classification Test score of over 110 – the required score to attend Officer Candidate School. A temporary Casual Detachment was formed to house and process fillers.

The glider infantry regiments and artillery battalions were not the only units deliverable by glider. All other divisional elements were also to be delivered this way. Unlike paratroopers, glider troops were involuntarily

---

3 Two of the Iwo Jima flag-raisers were former paratroopers.

11th Airborne Division, 1943

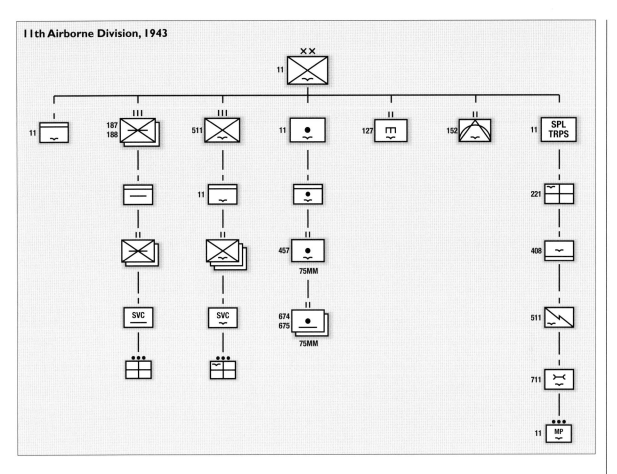

assigned to the units, and they received no hazardous duty or flight pay. Those unfortunate enough to be prone to airsickness or with a fear of flying were eventually transferred to other units. The paratroopers were another matter, as those who volunteered for jump training were assigned to parachute units. Unlike the earlier regiments assigned to the 82d and 101st AbnDivs, the parachute units assigned to the 11th were not yet parachute qualified. Swing also had a policy of encouraging all troops to undertake parachute training, which helped prevent a certain cocky and rebellious attitude that was prevalent among many of the volunteers.

Most of the component units were activated on February 25, but some had been organized earlier. The 511th PIR and 457th PFAB were activated on January 5 at Camp Toccoa, GA and Ft Bragg, NC respectively. The 457th soon joined the 511th at Toccoa, and they relocated to Camp Mackall on February 21. The 408th Airborne Quartermaster and 711th Airborne Ordnance Maintenance companies were activated prior to the division, on November 12, at Camp Gruber, OK and Miller Field, NY, respectively. The division's two bands were National Guard bands: 11th AbnDiv Artillery Band and the 511th PIR Band. The 713th Airborne Ordnance Maintenance Company was activated on May 15, 1943, attached to the 11th AbnDiv for administration, and assigned to the 13th AbnDiv on July 15.

As the units were filled, the new recruits spent their first weeks learning how to make bunks and stow their uniforms and equipment, executing basic drill, undergoing physical conditioning, and clearing and preparing training areas. The basic training phase began on March 15. The basic skills taught included drill, military courtesies, bayonet, hand-to-hand combat, field sanitation, first aid, chemical warfare defense, weaponry, and marksmanship, among others.

The shoulder sleeve insignia of the 11th Airborne Division indicates why the division was nicknamed "The Angels."

Between May and June the parachute units were sent to Ft Benning, GA one battalion at a time for three weeks' parachute training. The artillery battalions traveled to nearby Ft Bragg, NC for range firing, and the antiaircraft battalion spent two weeks at Ft Fisher, NC for gunnery training. Physical conditioning continued through all phases of training in the form of daily calisthenics, forced marches with full equipment, and unit runs.

The unit training program began on June 21. This included transition firing, infiltration, and close combat courses and live fire exercises for the infantry units. Platoon proficiency tests were conducted at Ft Bragg, NC. Service and support units were welded into functional teams. The parachute units executed progressively larger jumps from squad level upwards. The artillery battalions returned to Ft Bragg, NC for additional live fire training. The glider units went to Laurenburg-Maxton Army Airbase, NC for glider training. The artillery battalions were paired with the infantry regiments – the 457th PFAB with the 511th PIR, and the 674th and 675th Glider Field Artillery Battalions (GFAB) with the 187th and 188th Glider, respectively. Engineer companies were also paired with regiments. By October the battalion exercises were being conducted with accompanying units.

All tactical live fire and field training involves an element of risk, but the nature of airborne operations inflicted above-average casualties on the units. While at Mackall the division lost 16 men to glider and aircraft crashes.

The Secretary of War visited the division in late November and viewed a successful parachute and glider assault demonstration. However, the fierce debate over the future of the airborne divisions was reaching a decisive point. The marginal performance of US airborne units in North Africa and Sicily led many officers, including some airborne officers, to recommend the divisions be disbanded and only battalions be employed, formed into temporary task forces. To test the validity of the airborne concept and determine what the problem areas were and how to fix them, the Swing Board was convened by the War Department. A test maneuver was planned using the 11th AbnDiv, augmented by the 501st PIR and 874th Airborne Engineer Battalion, as the attacking force. The defending maneuver "enemy" was built around a regimental combat team of the 17th AbnDiv reinforced by a battalion of 541st PIR. The exercise was controlled by the Combined Airborne-Troop Carrier Maneuver Headquarters, co-directed by Brig Gen Fredrick W. Evans commanding I TC Command and Brig Gen Leo Donovan of the Airborne Command. The troops were unaware that the future of the airborne depended on the exercise's outcome. The Secretary of War and the Chief of the Army Ground Forces, Lt Gen Lesley M. McNair, would both be present for the exercise.

The Knollwood Maneuvers, as the exercise was known, took place December 6–11, 1943; weather delayed their start for a day. The primary objective for the attacking force was the Knollwood Airport and three other airports in north–central North Carolina. The mission assigned to the 11th AbnDiv was a tough one, deemed impossible by many. The parachute and glider regiments, with their support units, were to depart from several different airfields in eastern North Carolina; fly designated routes for 3–4 hours (some 200 miles) over the Atlantic at night in severe winter conditions with rain, fog, low clouds, and wind; deliver the assault force by parachute and glider at precise times and locations; assemble, and move to and seize multiple objectives. The airborne force then had to be kept resupplied entirely by airdrop and airlanding. Setting aside the absence of live ammunition, this exercise was even more challenging than some actual combat operations undertaken. The 53d TC Wing employed 200 C-47s and 234 CG-4A gliders to deliver 10,282 men – by parachute (4,679), glider (1,869), or airlanding (3,734) – along with 295 ¼-ton trucks, 274 ¼-ton trailers, and 326 tons of supplies. Training accidents resulted in two deaths and 48 injuries. The exercise was a complete success and all requirements

11th Airborne Division, 1944–45

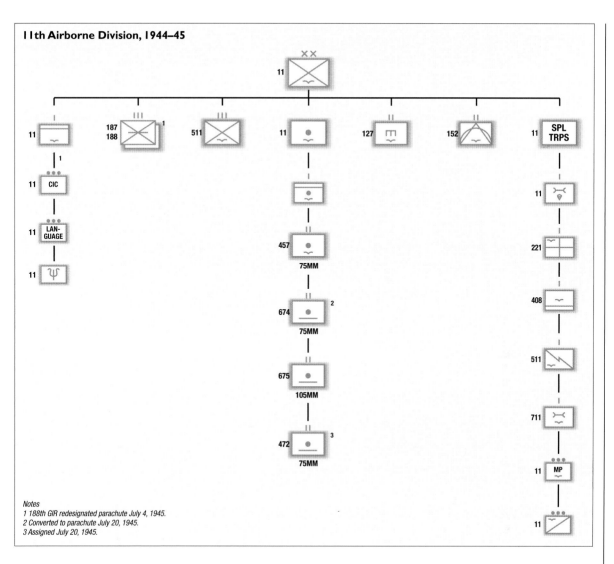

Notes
1 188th GIR redesignated parachute July 4, 1945.
2 Converted to parachute July 20, 1945.
3 Assigned July 20, 1945.

and objectives were met. After reviewing Swing's report and those of the observers, McNair sent a letter to Swing assuring him of the future of the five airborne divisions:

> I congratulate you on the splendid performance of your division in the Knollwood maneuver. After the airborne operations in Africa and Sicily, my staff and I had become convinced of the impartibility of handling large airborne units. I was prepared to recommend to the War Department that airborne divisions be abandoned in our scheme of organization and that the airborne effort be restricted to parachute units of battalion and smaller size. The successful performance of your division has convinced me that we were wrong, and I shall now recommend that we continue our present schedule of activating, training, and committing airborne divisions.

Rumors soon spread among members of the 11th AbnDiv that they were to be shipped overseas, but they were in fact bound for Camp Polk, LA. The entire division was moved by train between January 2 and 8, 1944. The division continued training, and conducted individual proficiency testing, a series of three-day exercises, followed by more unit tests. Glider training was conducted at DeRidder Army Airfield 20 miles to the south and a unit jump school was established there. Swing's goal was to make the division both parachute and glider capable. As a result, some glider troops were given parachute training, but they did not receive jump pay and were not allowed distinctive parachute insignia and uniform items; some of these volunteers were reassigned to parachute units. The paratroopers in turn received orientation on gliders, but took few, if any, flights. Training resources and time were simply not available for such extensive cross-training. Following a notification for overseas deployment, more training, tests, inspections, and inoculations were carried out, and new equipment issued. The March 15 departure date was delayed a month, which was filled with more training.

The division began boarding trains on April 20, 1944, and by the 28th the entire division had arrived at Camp Stoneman, CA. Here each unit spent six days undergoing processing, more inoculations, more equipment issue, and preparation for life on board ship. The units began moving by train to San Francisco on May 2. The division arrived at Milne Bay on the east end of Papua New Guinea at the end of May. With all the ships assembled they continued up the northeast coast and the division debarked at Buna-Dobodura, where a large tent camp was erected. Swing had first reported to General MacArthur in Australia while the 11th was en route, and as each unit arrived at their new camp he briefed them on MacArthur's plan for the division.

Once the camp was established training began anew and the jump school became operational. Those who had not completed this at Ft Polk went through the first courses, followed by volunteers from non-parachute units. This was considered an important process, as it was known that few gliders were available. Transports were in short supply as well, but at least some would be available for parachute operations. Swing wanted the glider units at least partly parachute qualified in order to be deployable in the event that the 511th was already committed and another parachute operation needed to be mounted. At one time 75 percent of the enlisted men and 82 percent of the officers were parachute qualified. Other unit schools were established including demolitions, communications, and patrolling. Some troops also attended Sixth Army schools including the Alamo Scout Training Center and a jungle training course operated by Australians familiar with New Guinea. The division was warned of a possible operation in western New Guinea, but it was canceled. In August and September sufficient gliders were delivered to allow a glider school to be operated by the 54th TC Wing at Nadzab, New Guinea. At the same time amphibious training was provided by the 4th Engineer Special Brigade at Oro Bay. From July to September troop carrier squadrons from the wing practiced dropping troops in jumps as a means of refining their own skills.

In late September the division began loading up nine transports, and departed on October 12 for Leyte in the central Philippines. The Sixth Army landed on the east–central coast of Leyte on October 20 with four divisions. The 11th did not arrive until November 18, when it executed an unopposed landing at Bito on the east coast, south of the original landing beaches.

503d Parachute Regimental Combat Team

The 503d PIR was organized from existing parachute units at Ft Benning, GA on March 2, 1942 – the first operational parachute regiment. Its 1st and 2d battalions had been created on February 24, being derived from the 503d and 504th Parachute Infantry battalions (PIB). These two battalions had been organized on August 22 and October 5, 1941, respectively, at Ft Benning, GA. The battalions were not "redesignated," but "consolidated" with the newly activated regimental battalions. The 3d Battalion was activated at Ft Bragg on June 8, 1942 from the 502d PIB. The regiment relocated to Ft Bragg on March 21 and was assigned to the Airborne Command. In July 1942 the 2d Battalion departed for Scotland, the first airborne unit to be deployed overseas; it was selected because of its advanced state of training. There it was redesignated 2d Battalion, 509th PIR on November 2 and eventually became the 509th PIB.

Despite speculation that the rest of the regiment would follow, its ranks were filled with jump school graduates and men drawn from other parachute units, and sent by train to Camp Stoneman, CA in mid October 1942. It departed aboard a Dutch freighter, MS *Poelau Laut*, on the 19th. The ship made port at Panama and embarked the 501st Parachute Battalion. This was the Army's first parachute unit raised on September 16, 1940 at Ft Benning as the 1st Parachute Battalion. It was redesignated 501st Parachute Battalion on October 1 ("Infantry" was never included in its title). It provided cadres for three new battalions in the last half of 1941 – 502d, 503d, and 504th. On October 30 the 501st departed for the Panama Canal Zone; its Company C had preceded it, and was stationed at Ft Kobbe on the Pacific side. There the unit was filled with volunteers. Its Company C was absorbed into 1st Battalion, 551st PIR, activated there in November 1942. The 501st Battalion commander, Lt Col William M. Miley, retuned to the States to take command of the new 503d PIR and Maj Kenneth Kinsler assumed command. Kinsler also returned to the States to become the Executive Officer (XO) of the 503d PIR and soon its commander. The 501st's XO, Maj George M. Jones, took over the battalion. In the Canal Zone the battalion served as part of the defense force, stood by for contingency operations in the Caribbean, filled up with volunteers recruited locally giving them parachute training, and conducted jungle exercises. The two-company 501st embarked aboard the *Poelau Laut* at the end of October and the ship proceeded to Australia arriving in Cairns,

Col George M. Jones, commander of the 503d Parachute Regimental Combat Team, and his staff plan the February 1945 Corregidor jump. Meticulous planning was essential for airborne operations, but once on the ground units had to be highly flexible.

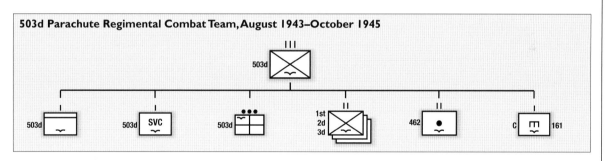

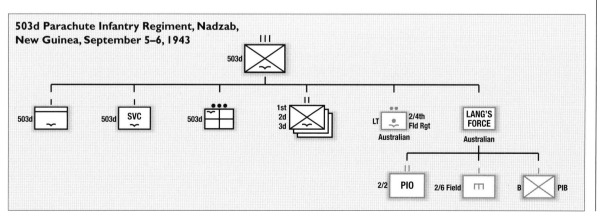

The unofficial shoulder sleeve insignia of the 503d Parachute Regimental Combat Team depicts a parachuting wildcat.

Queensland on December 6. On November 2, 1942 the 501st was formally inactivated and 2d Battalion, 503d PIR activated.[4] Company A, 504th PIR detached from the 82d AbnDiv had accompanied the 503d to Panama and was absorbed into the new 2d Battalion as its Company D.

The 1,939-man (authorized 1,958) 503d PIR established Camp Cable at Gordonvale, Australia. The men conducted extensive jungle training in the dense forests there, experimented with jumping weapons and equipment, and developed tactics. Much personnel reshuffling took place in order to put the right people in the right positions. After eight months of intense training the unit was more than ready for action. This included training at the demanding Australian Land Headquarters Training Centre (Jungle Warfare) at Canungra in southeast Queensland. The unit was alerted for the Nadzab jump on New Guinea in the first week of August 1943.

Following the Noemfoor Island jump the 503d PIR received two augmentation units to become the 503d Parachute Regimental Combat Team at the end of August. The 462d PFAB[5] had been activated at Camp

---

[4] The 501st Parachute Infantry Battalion itself was never redesignated 1st Battalion, 501st Parachute Infantry, as implied in that unit's lineage. The latter was a new unit activated at Camp Toccoa, GA in November 1942.

[5] The unit was officially designated 462d Field Artillery Battalion (FAB) and though organized under a PFAB T/O&E, it never bore this designation, although it was called such and will continue to be so in this book to prevent confusion.

Australian 1 Parachute Battalion

The Australian parachute unit owed its existence to the decision made by the War Cabinet on June 10, 1941, which asked if the Army had considered parachute troops. The Chief of the Air Staff reported that the only suitable aircraft, Hudsons, were needed for reconnaissance work. The Army indicated that it could undertake preliminary ground training and this was directed to begin in July. Even though the concept was supported by the Minister for the Army, many of the senior Army leadership were less than enthusiastic and slow in implementing the effort.

A Parachute Training Unit was formed at Laverton, Victoria in November 1942 and soon moved to Tocumwal Aerodrome, New South Wales. Limited recruiting began in October 1942, but it was not until December that 40 volunteers began training. Most volunteers came from independent (commando) companies. The administrative staff, physical training staff,

and female parachute packers were Royal Australian Air Force (RAAF) while the instructors were Army trained by the RAAF. Aircraft were limited to one each DC-2 and Wirraway. The course required four jumps and the first class graduated at the end of January 1943. In April the Parachute Training Unit was moved to Richmond RAAF Station near Sydney owing to more favorable weather conditions. Besides training troops for the planned parachute battalion, supporting artillerymen and engineers were trained along with independent companies, Z Special Unit, and Dutchmen, Indians, Javanese and Malayans for special operations. British parachute training methods were implemented and seven jumps were now required. More aircraft were available in the form of C-47 Dakotas.

A Company, 1 Parachute Battalion was formed at Richmond on April 19, 1943. It contained a headquarters, three platoons, and a 3in. mortar section, and undertook tactical training and raised cadres for future companies. It focused on night, jungle, and water jumps, given the tactical necessities of the Southwest Pacific. No reserve parachutes were used and several fatalities occurred. B Company and Headquarters Company were formed on August 9 and the battalion itself on the 15th. The following month the battalion moved to Scheyville, New South Wales. C Company was formed in October 1943 and D Company in June 1944. The battalion had a Battalion Headquarters, Headquarters Company, A–D Companies,

Reinforcement Company (rear base), and the Royal Australian Engineer Parachute Troop.

In June 1944 the battalion moved to Mareeba, Queensland to prepare for its first mission. Operation *Kingfisher* was a plan to rescue Australian prisoners of war on Borneo if the Japanese began massacring them. Australian troops were landing on Borneo and special forces were operating in the interior. Even though MacArthur supported the plan and ample aircraft and landing craft were available, Gen Sir Thomas Blamey, Commander-in-Chief, Australian Military Forces, ordered the battalion to stand down for two weeks' leave. They were never employed for rescue operations, not even to intervene in the January–June 1945 Sandakan Death Marches in which hundreds of Australians died. Morale plummeted and troops requested transfers, but were denied. A second battalion was planned and the two battalions were projected to take Singapore alongside British paras, but the war's end canceled its formation. A 120-man company-size element of the battalion deployed to Singapore and participated in the September surrender. It served as an honor guard until returned to Sydney in late January 1946. The rest of the battalion and the Parachute Training Unit had already been disbanded after the war's end. The remainder was disbanded at Ingleburn Camp on January 30, 1946 without seeing combat or making operational jumps. (Insignia courtesy of Harry Pugh, Chute and Dagger.)

Mackall on June 16, 1943 with a cadre from the 458th PFAB. The 462d departed San Francisco on March 12, 1944 arriving in Australia on the 29th. It was assigned the 503d PIR on March 29, but would not join the regiment until late August. The 562d trained at Camp Cable until it was shipped to Noemfoor in August, where it provided fire support. The other unit was Company C (Parachute), 161st Airborne Engineer Battalion. The battalion had been activated as the 161st Engineer Squadron at Ft Bliss, TX. It was redesignated an airborne engineer battalion May 1, 1943 at Camp Carson, CO and its Company C (Parachute) was detached and reassigned to the Airborne Command on October 18, never to rejoin the battalion. It was sent to Laurinburg-Maxton, NC then to Ft Benning, GA for jump training at the end of 1943. It returned briefly to Maxton then went to Camp Mackall, CA. It departed California on April 26, arrived at Milne Bay, Papua New Guinea in mid May, and then shipped to Noemfoor in August for assignment to the 503d on September 13.

541st Parachute Infantry Regiment

The 541st PIR was organized at Ft Benning, GA on August 12, 1943 from recent graduates of the Parachute Course. Col Ducat M. McEntee commanded the regiment through its three-year existence. It was relocated to Camp Mackall, NC on October 14 where it conducted demonstration exercises, tested equipment, and developed tactics and techniques for other parachute units. One battalion participated in the December 1943 Knollwood Maneuvers. On March 1, 1944 it was assigned to XVIII Airborne Corps and stripped of most of its personnel for overseas replacements. On July 29 it moved back to Ft Benning, GA where its cadre was assigned to the Replacement and School Command. There it served as a training unit, conducting the 13-week parachute infantryman program for troops before they undertook the Parachute Course. They were then dispatched as replacements. On November 16, 1944 it was reattached to the Airborne Center and returned to Camp Mackall, NC on the 23rd. There it was brought up to full strength and conducted extensive overseas deployment training for assignment to the 11th AbnDiv. Airborne divisions were now to have only one glider and two parachute regiments, and it was envisioned the 541st would become the 11th's second parachute regiment. It traveled by train to Camp Stoneman, CA, arriving on May 23, 1945, and departed for the Philippines on June 5.

Arriving at Manila on July 10, the regiment was devastated to learn it would be broken up. Rather than inactivate one of the two glider regiments with one of its two battalions becoming the new 3d Battalion of the other, the 187th and 188th had formed cadre 3d Battalions and the 541st was absorbed into battalions of all three original regiments, which were in desperate need of replacements after the Luzon campaign. The 541st was officially inactivated on August 10 at Lipa, Luzon. While disappointing to the men of the 541st, who had trained together long and hard, the decision made sense. It allowed Swing to come closer to his goal of making his three regiments both parachute and glider capable. The 188th Glider Infantry Regiment (GIR) was redesignated 188th PIR on July 20, being filled out with paratroopers from the 541st. Swing hoped that in the future the 187th GIR, which now contained a high percentage of parachute-qualified troops, would also become dual capable. His decision made sense, because the division was preparing for the invasion of Japan and he preferred to retain his three combat-experienced regiments and their leadership rather than break one up and replace it with a green unit. While the 541st never saw action, its contributions to tactical development, replacement training, and revitalizing the 11th AbnDiv was invaluable to the war effort.

Parachute Section, 5217th/ 1st Reconnaissance Battalion
The 5217th Reconnaissance Battalion (Provisional) was formed in November 1943 in Australia under MacArthur's General Headquarters (see Battle Orders 12: *US Special Warfare Units in the Pacific Theater 1941–45*.) Its mission was to infiltrate small parties of Filipinos and Americans by submarine into the Philippines to contact guerrilla bands, assess them, provide advice and support, establish intelligence nets, and report intelligence to GHQ. The battalion's motto was *Bahala Na – Tagalong* ("Come What May!") A Parachute Section was established in May 1944 at Camp Tabragalba, Australia with the aid of three 503d PIR paratroopers under 1st Lt Earl Walter. This would give the unit the capability to airdrop parties into the Philippines. However, while 66 men were jump qualified, no parties were delivered by parachute. In November, 1944 the 5217th was reorganized as the 1st Reconnaissance Battalion, Special. While the Parachute Section was based at Hollandia, Netherlands New Guinea a transport crashed in the jungle. On May 18, 1945, two men parachuted in to check for survivors. Twenty-one died, but there were three critically injured. On the 20th nine more men jumped into a valley, hacked out a landing strip, and walked to the crash site over ten miles away. After 42 days and resupplied by airdrop, the survivors recovered sufficiently to walk to the valley and were lifted out by three CG-5A gliders picked up by C-47 tugs on July 2.

Training

While there were differences, the fundamentals of Marine and Army parachute training were similar. Here Marines practice parachute landing falls off a low platform into a sawdust pit.

US airborne training, doctrine, and tactics have already been discussed in detail in Battle Orders 22 and 25. The discussion of training, doctrine, and tactics here will focus on the aspects that applied to the PTO, whose terrain and climate, and where the enemy's tactics and airlift problems created a very different environment to Europe and the Mediterranean.

A squad of Marine paratroopers prepare for a practice jump. They are armed with .45-cal. M55 Reising submachine guns, which were secured behind their reserve parachutes during a jump. Most jumps in the Pacific were from less than 500ft and reserve chutes were unnecessary. Nonetheless, they were retained on the off chance they might have time to open, but also to protect the jumper's torso if landing in a tree.

The 511th PIR, for example, was organized from volunteers who completed basic infantry and other specialist training within the unit, the 13-week basic Parachute Infantry Training Program. They then attended the three-week Parachute Course at Ft Benning, GA by rotating battalions. The 503d PIR was organized from existing parachute units, and the original members had been trained within their units. Additional personnel were either transferred from other parachute units or undertook the 13-week basic infantry training at a replacement training center. Ft Benning, GA also provided the 13-week infantry program, along with demolitions and communications training. Replacements, already trained as infantrymen or other specialists, volunteered from other units as well. A small percentage of replacements were obtained by accepting volunteers from within the theater of operations. These individuals were trained by unit-operated jump schools.

Unit training was progressively conducted through company, battalion, and regimental levels over 13 weeks. This was followed by 13 weeks of combined training in which regimental combat teams undertook exercises with attached artillery, antiaircraft, antitank, engineer, and other support units, and then a division exercise.

Joint training conducted by airborne and troop carrier units was deemed essential. In such complex operations a high degree of familiarity between the two organizations was essential. It was not adequate for a troop carrier unit to train with one airborne unit and then be deployed to operate with another unit. Units had to be confident in each other's abilities. In the PTO the 54th TC Wing's 317th TC Group conducted most airborne operations. There were still problems because of the rotation of trained air crews and insufficient time to train new crews. Changes in tactical plans once an operation commenced also caused problems, but such changes could not always be avoided.

An Army 250ft jump tower at Ft. Benning, GA. The jumper was hoisted by a cable and released to drift free to the ground, thus gaining experience in steering and landing. Only one or two arms of the tower were used, depending on wind direction.

Airlift units

USAAF troop carrier (TC) units were organized into TC wings of 2–4 TC groups. TC groups had four TC squadrons of 18 C-47s each and augmented by 18 or 36 CG-4A gliders if available. All parachute operations conducted in the PTO were supported by the 54th TC Wing comprising the 2d Combat Cargo (1944–46),

317th TC (1943–46), 374th TC (1943), 375th TC (1943–46), and 433d TC (1943–46) Groups. They provided troop lift, parachute drop, and glider towing, carried supplies and equipment, dropped supplies to guerrillas, evacuated casualties, and performed many unusual missions: the 317th TC Group bombed Caraao Island in Manila Bay with napalm

drums. The wing was activated at Brisbane, Australia on February 13, 1943 and inactivated in Manila on May 31, 1946.

All airborne operations were supported by the 317th TC Group with the exception of Los Baños, which was dropped by the 433d. The 317th's TC squadrons were the 39th, 40th, 41st, and 46th. 317th TC Group commanders during the period when airborne operations were conducted were Col Samuel V. Payne (February 22, 1942), Col Robert L. Olinger (June 21, 1944), and Col John H. Lackey, Jr. (October 2, 1944).

A Marine utility squadron (VMJ – the "V" means heavier-than-air, the "M" Marine, and the third letter is a code for the type of squadron) had 12–15 R4D transports, three utility transports, and three utility airplanes. The utility aircraft were used for liaison, search and rescue, and personnel and parts delivery, etc. In June/July 1944 the eight squadrons were redesignated Marine transport squadrons (VMR) and now had only 12 R4Ds – VMJ/VMR-152, 153, 252, 253, 352, 353, 952, 953. The few squadrons actually deployed in the PTO were subordinate to Marine Aircraft Group 25 (MAG-25).

Guidelines for training airborne divisions were released on November 2, 1943 in the Army Ground Forces memorandum, *Joint Training of Airborne and Troop Carrier Units*. It laid out a new program of joint training for parachute units from battalion to division levels. It specified three phases: small unit (battalion), large unit (regiment), and division. The tasks, condition, and standards for each phase were spelt out, with each phase building on the previous. It also listed the requirements airborne divisions were to satisfy before Army Ground Forces certified them combat ready. It was a demanding standard, but all airborne divisions accomplished it prior to deployment.

A Marine paratrooper practices spilling air from an inflated canopy. At the time there were no quick-release devices allowing a canopy to be jettisoned if a jumper was dragged along the ground – a dangerous situation.

1. Five-day division exercise.
2. Deploy from at least four airbases.
3. Objective area had to be reached flying a circuitous route of approximately 300 miles.
5. At least half of the parachute and glider landings to be made at night.
6. Contact with friendly ground forces would not be made before D+4.
7. All resupply and evacuation to be made by air or air-landing from D-Day to D+4.

Once deployed overseas, training continued and often intensified. Units acclimatized to the environment through forced marches, land navigation exercises in rugged tropical terrain, weapons and equipment training, range firing, organized athletics, and unit exercises at all echelons. Staff collected information on enemy forces and tactics. Paratroopers commonly received training on enemy weapons. Rubber boat training and amphibious exercises using Army engineer special brigade landing craft were also conducted, as these were an alternative means of introduction to the battlefield in the PTO.

The 503d arrived in Australia in early December 1942 and conducted eight months' training before the Nadzab jump on New Guinea. They then had two more months of training time until Noemfoor, followed by another three months until Mindoro, after which they were either engaged or redeploying to new combat zones until almost the war's end. The 11th AbnDiv arrived in the PTO in June 1944 and undertook three and a half months of training before being sent to Leyte. The 11th subsequently deployed to Leyte or Luzon with only brief rest spells until May 1945, before being completely reorganized and retrained until deploying to Japan at the end of August.

The Marines used a 135ft tower on which the descending parachute remained attached to guide cables. This type of tower originated as an amusement park ride introduced at the 1939 New York World's Fair.

Marine paratroopers land during a practice jump. On level ground clear of obstacles, and in less than 15 mph winds, the chance of injury was minimal. Of course, the mission dictated where jumps would be made and available DZs usually featured far from ideal conditions.

Doctrine

A Marine paratrooper hanging in a tree. While risky, this often did not result in injury. The most dangerous part was getting out of the tree. Jumpers typically carried 30–40ft of rope. They could also open their reserve chute, lower the deflated canopy, and climb down it, ensuring they did not climb into the canopy.

The US Army's airborne doctrine evolved through the war as lessons were learned, capabilities improved, and new units were fielded. There was no official codified doctrine above regimental level. The only formal document published during the war was Field Manual 31-30, *Tactics and Techniques of Air-Borne Troops, May 20, 1942,* which served through the war. When it was released the first four parachute regiments were in the process of being organized, and no exercises above battalion size had taken place. Field Manual 100-5, *Field Service Regulations: Operations, May 22, 1941* only provided minimal guidance for the employment of airborne forces by higher commands, and a more complete manual was not issued until 1944. Various studies and directives were issued by higher commands though, and these incorporated lessons learned as airborne operations were executed and according to the needs of the situation.

Initial doctrine saw paratroopers as commandos or raiders operating in units of no more than battalion size, sometimes even as companies or platoons operating independently. They would conduct harassing raids, demolitions in the enemy's rear, and sabotage, before fading away into the hills to fight as guerrillas if unable to link up with ground forces. They were seen as a means to achieve victory sooner with fewer costs in time, manpower, and resources. The reality was that such small-scale operations had little impact on the enemy, while expending highly trained troops. It was realized that airborne troops needed to be employed in larger units with organic firepower to deliver a significant punch behind enemy lines and inflict damage on him. They had to be employed boldly, but with skill and imagination.

After the early airborne operations in North Africa, Sicily, and Italy, the Swing Board was established to examine doctrine, problems encountered during actual operations, and make recommendations for improvements. As a result, the War Department published new guidelines in the form of Training Circular (TC) 113, *Employment of Airborne and Troop Carrier Forces, October 9, 1943.* TC 113 specified nine basic missions for airborne units:

1. To seize hold, or otherwise exploit important tactical localities in conjunction with or pending the arrival of other naval or military forces.

Originally all paratroopers were taught to pack parachutes, but this required additional training time, attention to detail, and frequent practice to maintain proficiency. By 1942 specialist parachute riggers packed, maintained, and repaired parachutes, freeing paratroopers of the task and ensuring parachutes were properly packed.

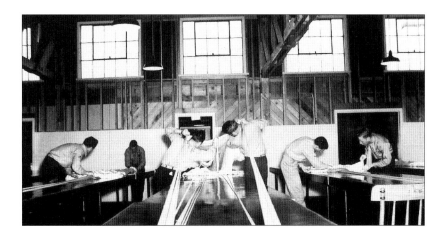

2. To attack the enemy rear and assist the breakthrough or landing by the main force.
3. To reinforce threatened or surrounded units.
4. To seize islands or areas which were not strongly held and which the enemy could not easily reinforce.
5. To capture enemy airfields.
6. To capture and destroy vital enemy installations and thus paralyze the enemy's system of command, communications, and supply.
7. To create diversions.
8. To assist the tactical air forces in delaying retreating enemy forces until the main ground forces could destroy them.
9. To create confusion and disorder among hostile military and civil personnel.

The existing principles were considered mostly sound by airborne commanders throughout the war. Extensions and modifications were made in practice to accommodate tactical situations, the terrain, enemy capabilities, and resource limitations, especially with regard to airlift assets.

Recognizing that airborne operations in North Africa, Sicily, and Italy had experienced severe difficulties, TC 113 cited the 503d PIR's Nadzab operation as the only one to date exhibiting proper planning and execution.

It stated that airborne and troop carrier units were theater of operation forces, and the controlling headquarters could coordinate all involved ground, sea, and air forces. The airborne unit remained under the direct control of the theater commander until it landed in the combat area, at which point it passed to the control of the ground commander. Another principle dealt with the missions that units were to conduct; airborne units were specially trained and equipped to accomplish a specific mission, and were not to be utilized for missions that could be performed by other units. Once passed to the control of the ground commander, the mission of an airborne unit was to be limited to its initial objectives. It would be relieved by a ground unit, which would continue the operations while the airborne unit returned to base.

Airborne units were also to land rapidly *en masse*, within a relatively small area. The piecemeal dropping of troops over a period of days, as seen in Sicily, was to be avoided, as was scattering them over a large area in small, difficult to support units. The limited number of aircraft meant that subsequent regimental drops allowed for only one battalion at a time to be dropped with the other battalions delivered by follow-on lifts. It also recommended that dedicated aircraft be used for resupply drops and not just the troop jump aircraft reused. This prevented confusion with loads and timing.

Once dropped in, parachute units relied heavily on parachute resupply drops. A considerable amount of manpower was required to recover supplies from DZs as there were usually no vehicles available. Here members of the 511th PIR bring in ammunition crates from the DZ. Parachute canopies were often used as shelters from the blistering sun and as a form of camouflage "net," as later canopies were olive drab or camouflage patterned.

Well-equipped combat surgical teams were dropped in during parachute assaults. Even serious casualties could not be evacuated until an airstrip was opened in the airhead. Casualties relied on para-surgeons to keep them alive.

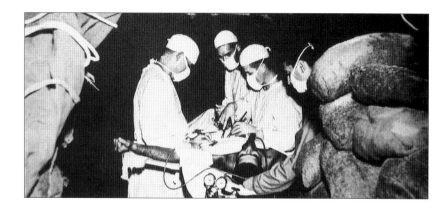

An essential principle was the airborne unit's complete integration into the maneuver plan. To be fully effective, it could not be added on or superimposed onto a plan. Likewise, an airborne operation could not be conducted on its own without being part of a larger operation. The airborne operation had to contribute something concrete to the maneuver plan. Gen Swing commented:

> Commanders must refrain from assigning airborne missions merely because airborne troops are available, and commit them only at appropriate times on missions suitable to their capabilities, limitations and available supporting means.

Another essential principle was that airborne forces should not be inserted in enemy territory unless it was certain that ground or sea forces could link up with them within three days. Longer than this would result in high casualties and require a huge and risky effort to keep the force resupplied by air, which in turn would deny airlift assets to other units. However, it also meant that airborne forces could not be deployed to a strategic depth, as envisioned by generals Marshall and Arnold – an impractical goal in any case, as it would be extremely difficult to resupply and support deep inside enemy territory, and would have limited heavy weapons and motor transport to move them and other supplies. Casualty evacuation would be almost impossible. The force would have to remain essentially stationary, relying on ammunition and supplies to be delivered to it. How deep a force could be inserted all depended on the range and loiter time of the supporting aircraft.

Another valuable aspect of the presence of airborne units in a theater of operations was that the enemy had to allocate units and resources and dispense its forces to protect vital installations within the ever-growing reach of American airbases.

PTO parachute operations			
Location	Date	Force size	Mission
Nadzab, New Guinea	5 Sep 1943	Regiment	Seize airfield, block enemy withdrawal.
Noemfoor Island	3–4 Jul 1944	Regiment (less elements)	Reinforcement.
Manarawat, Leyte	1 Dec 1944	Artillery battery	Position artillery.
Tagaytay Ridge, Luzon	3–4 Feb 1945	Regiment (less elements)	Seize dominating terrain.
Corregidor Island, Philippines	16 Feb 1945	Regiment (less elements)	Seize island.
Los Baños, Luzon	23 Feb 1945	Company (reinforced)	Liberate internees.
Netherlands New Guinea	18/20 May 1945	Team	Rescue crash survivors.
Camalaniugan, Luzon	23 Jun 1945	Battalion (reinforced)	Block enemy withdrawal.

Unit organization

While it was originally proposed for airborne divisions to be manned to levels similar to an infantry division and with a similar allocation of weapons, Army Ground Forces directed that they would be kept very small and light, comprising 8,400 troops as compared to 14,043. They possessed only the strength and armament necessary for short-term missions. They were especially lean in service support assets, not even enough for routine garrison and training support.[6]

Unit designation practices

Parachute infantry regiments consisted of three battalions (1st–3d) and glider infantry regiments two (1st and 2d) with a third added in late 1944/45. The regiment's companies were lettered in sequence: 1st Battalion – A–C, 2d – D–F, and 3d – G–I. The regimental service company was simply Service Company, 503d PIR. Parachute rifle platoons were designated 1st–3d Platoons, Company A, 511th PIR, for example. A parachute rifle platoon's squads were designated 1st, 2d, and Mortar Squads, 1st Platoon. Glider companies had only two rifle platoons (1st and 2d) with three rifle squads (1st–3d). Parachute field artillery battalions' batteries were designated batteries A–D. Glider artillery battalions had only two batteries.

The Marine parachute battalions were simply numbered 1st–4th and retained these designations when assigned to the 1st Parachute Regiment. Being a special unit it was not numbered with the normal series of Marine regiments (1st–29th Marines), which included infantry, artillery, and engineer regiments. As separate battalions their companies were identified as A–C. When the regiment was organized the companies were redesignated in sequence through the regiment: 1st Battalion – A–C, 2d Battalion – E–G, 3d Battalion – I, K, L (no Company J), and 4th Battalion – N–P. Companies D, H, M, and Q were reserved in the event that battalion weapons companies were authorized at a later date.

11th Airborne Division organization

The 11th AbnDiv was activated under the October 15, 1942 Table of Organization (T/O&E) 71, as other divisions. It would retain this basic T/O until July 1945 when it prepared for the invasion of Japan and adopted a new T/O. All of its combat would be under this T/O as it did not reorganize under the December 1944 Table of Organization and Equipment (T/O&E)[7] as it was engaged in combat. By the time it was able to reorganize a new T/O&E had been introduced.

At Camp Polk, LA the parachute maintenance and supply platoon/sections of the 511th PIR, 457th PFAB, and 127th Airborne Engineer Battalion were consolidated into the Provisional Parachute Maintenance Company, 11th AbnDiv. A Provisional Reconnaissance Platoon, 11th AbnDiv was also organized, the "Killer" or "Ghost Platoon." The 11th Counterintelligence Corps Detachment and Language Detachment, 11th AbnDiv were added later. On New Guinea the two bands were consolidated into the 11th AbnDiv Infantry Band.

---

6 See Battle Orders 22 and 25 for further details on organizational aspects of US airborne forces in World War II. Aspects unique to the 11th AbnDiv, 503d PIR, and Marine parachute units are discussed in the section that follows.

7 Prior to 1943 two separate documents specified a unit's organization and equipage, the table of organization (T/O) and the table of basic allowances (T/BA) for unit and individual equipment. From mid 1942, as new types of units were created and existing units reorganized, the tables of equipment (T/E) began to replace the T/BA. The two documents were consolidated as the table of organization and equipment (T/O&E) by mid 1943.

11th Airborne Division, 1943	T/O
HQ, 11th AbnDiv	71-1
HQ Company, 11th AbnDiv	71-2
187th Glider Infantry Regiment	7-51
188th Glider Infantry Regiment	7-51
511th Parachute Infantry Regiment	7-31
127th Airborne Engineer Battalion	5-225
152d Airborne Antiaircraft Battalion	4-275
11th AbnDiv Artillery	6-200
HQ & HQ Battery	6-200-1
457th Parachute Field Artillery Battalion	6-215
674th Glider Field Artillery Battalion	6-255
675th Glider Field Artillery Battalion	6-255
Special Troops	
221st Airborne Medical Company	8-37
408th Airborne Quartermaster Company	10-327
511th Airborne Signal Company	11-557
711th Airborne Ordnance Maintenance Company	9-87
Military Police Platoon, 11th AbnDiv	19-97

The 511th PIR was organized into a headquarters and headquarters company with a regimental band, service company, medical detachment, and three infantry battalions. The battalions included a headquarters and headquarters company, medical detachment, and three rifle companies. Rifle companies had a small headquarters and three rifle platoons with a headquarters, two rifle squads, and a mortar squad. There was no battalion weapons company or company weapons platoon as in standard infantry units.

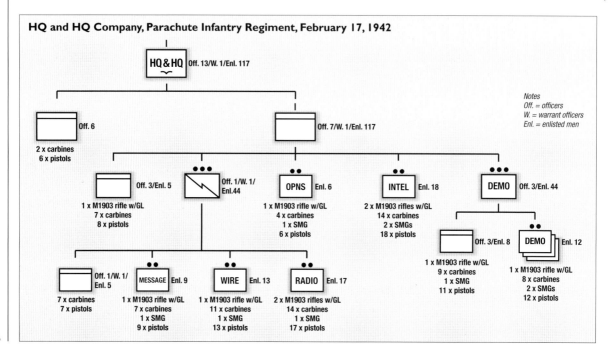

HQ and HQ Company, Parachute Infantry Regiment, February 17, 1942

Within the battalion headquarters company were a mortar platoon (4 x 81mm) and a light machine-gun (LMG) platoon (8 x .30-cal. LMGs). The regimental headquarters company possessed a demolition platoon with a section for attachment to each battalion. A platoon's two rifle squads each had a .30-cal. LMG plus two spares to be used in defensive situations. The platoon had a

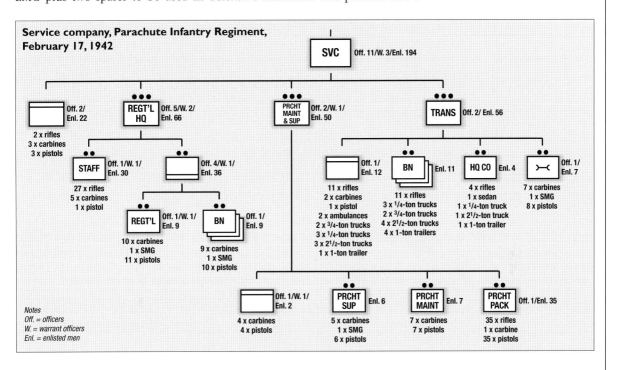

Service company, Parachute Infantry Regiment, February 17, 1942

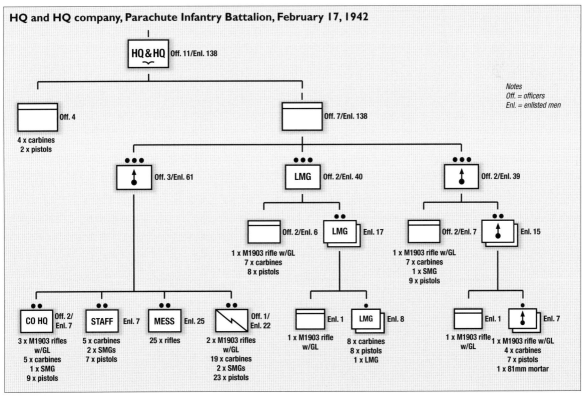

HQ and HQ company, Parachute Infantry Battalion, February 17, 1942

27

60mm mortar squad. Parachute rifle squads were not authorized Browning automatic rifles (BARs), but it appears in both the 11th AbnDiv and the 503d PIR they were often issued in lieu of the machine guns.

After the Nadzab operation the 503d PIR undertook a reorganization outside the T/O. The battalion eight-gun light machine-gun platoon was replaced by three four-gun platoons with one to be attached to each company. A third rifle squad was added to rifle platoons. Rifle squads now had a BAR and a rifle grenade launcher while the third squad had a light machine gun. A mortar platoon was organized from the former rifle platoon 60mm squads. Mortar squads could still be attached to rifle platoons if necessary. By the time of the Corregidor jump one of the mortar squads had a direct-fire, shoulder-fired mortar. The 503d did not receive bazookas until they were issued M9s in late 1944.

Organic weapons, Parachute Infantry Regiment, 1943–45				
Weapon	HQ & HQ Coy	Infantry battalion (x3)	Service Coy	Total
.30-cal. M1/M1903 rifle	15	340	138	1,173
.30-cal. M1 carbine	128	101	64	495
.45-cal. M1928A1 SMG	13	45	6	154
.45-cal. M1911A1 pistol	131	505	107	1,753
.30-cal. M1919A4 LMG	—	44	—	132
2.36in. M1/M1A1 rocket launcher	5	21	5	73
60mm M2 mortar	—	9	—	27
81mm M1 mortar	—	4	—	12
M1 grenade launcher	15	15	—	60

The two glider infantry regiments had a headquarters and headquarters company, service company, medical detachment, and two infantry battalions. The battalion included a headquarters and headquarters company, medical detachment, and three rifle companies. Rifle companies were composed of a headquarters, two rifle platoons with a headquarters and three rifle squads (each with a BAR), and a weapons platoon with two LMGs and two 60mm. The battalion headquarters company had a mortar platoon (6 x 81mm) and a heavy machine-gun (HMG) platoon (4 x HMGs). There was no regimental demolition platoon, but there were two antitank platoons (4 x 37mm each).

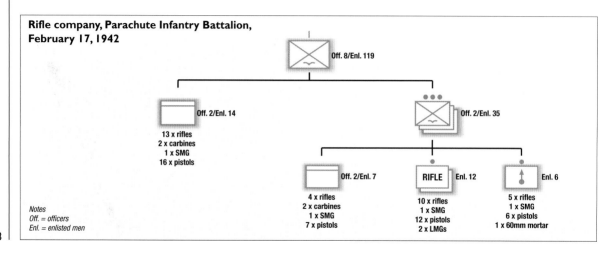

Rifle company, Parachute Infantry Battalion, February 17, 1942

Off. 8/Enl. 119

Off. 2/Enl. 14
13 x rifles
2 x carbines
1 x SMG
16 x pistols

Off. 2/Enl. 35

Off. 2/Enl. 7
4 x rifles
2 x carbines
1 x SMG
7 x pistols

RIFLE Enl. 12
10 x rifles
1 x SMG
12 x pistols
2 x LMGs

Enl. 6
5 x rifles
1 x SMG
6 x pistols
1 x 60mm mortar

Notes
Off. = officers
Enl. = enlisted men

Organic weapons, Glider Infantry Regiment, 1943–45

Weapon	HQ & HQ Coy	Infantry battalion (x2)	Service Coy	Total
.30-cal. M1/M1903 rifle	66	336	54	792
.30-cal. M1 carbine	149	231	24	635
.30-cal. M1918A2 BAR	—	18	6	42
.45-cal. M1911A1 pistol	19	58	1	136
.30-cal. M1919A4 LMG	—	6	—	12
.30-cal. M1917A1 HMG	—	4	—	8
.50-cal. M2 MG	—	—	3	3
37mm M3A1 AT gun	8	—	—	8
2.36-in. M1/M1A1 rocket launcher	2	30	10	72
60mm M2 mortar	—	12	—	24
81mm M1 mortar	—	6	—	12
M1 grenade launcher	16	46	12	120

The parachute field artillery battalion was organized into a headquarters and headquarters battery, medical detachment, three howitzer batteries (4 x 75mm), and an antiaircraft (AA) and antitank (AT) battery. Normally this battery had two AA platoons (4 x .50-cal. MGs) and two AT platoons (2 x 37mm).

However, the AA/AT battery (Battery D) was reorganized in both the 11th AbnDiv and 503d PIR. The 11th AbnDiv had little need for additional antitank guns and .50-cal. machine guns. On New Guinea it rearmed Battery D, 457th

1st Special Service Force
The FSSF was a combined US and Canadian unit, the latter making up just over a quarter of its strength. It was organized on July 9, 1942 at Ft William Harrison, MT for a somewhat questionable plan to parachute three commando forces into snow-covered regions of Norway, Romania, and Italy. The heavily armed forces would rely on small, full-tracked carriers known as Weasels and would be sustained by airdrop. Project *Plough* was wisely canceled later in the year. The number of aircraft required to deliver the hundreds of Weasels and sustain the force would have made it

impossible. The units would have had to have fuel, ammunition, and supplies dropped to them every few days. This would make the forces vulnerable and the enemy could easily have interdicted the transports. How much damage the small units could have inflicted was also questionable. With the original mission canceled the Force underwent a slight reorganization to make it more capable of undertaking normal combat operations. The FSSF was organized into three two-battalion regiments plus the Force Service Battalion. The regiments were smaller than a conventional infantry battalion. The unit was highly trained in small-unit and commando tactics, mountain climbing, skiing, snowshoeing, demolitions, hand-to-hand combat, weapons, etc. The one week of abbreviated parachute training with two jumps was completed in August by 1,200 forcemen. The FSSF undertook additional mountain and tactical training at Camp Ethan Allen, VT and then amphibious training at Norfolk, VA from April to June 1943. This included rubber boat training, which was to prove more useful than parachute training. The FSSF departed

San Francisco in July bound for Alaska's Aleutian Islands. Kiska Island was assaulted on August 15 with the FSSF's 1st Regiment landing on the opposite side of the island from the main east coast landing. The island's 6,000 Japanese had been secretly evacuated by July 28. The FSSF's 3d Regiment landed on neighboring Little Kiska the next day. The 2d Regiment was on standby to make a reinforcing jump onto southern Kiska if necessary. This was canceled. The FSSF returned to the States in September to depart for Morocco in November and then moved to Italy. It fought in the mountains of Italy, conducted an amphibious landing at Anzio in June 1944 and in August it conducted another amphibious assault off southern France. It fought there with the 1st Airborne Task Force until inactivated on November 23, 1944. No jump refresher or proficiency training was ever undertaken after their qualifying jumps. Replacements were not parachute qualified. When the unit was inactivated the few parachute-qualified troops were reassigned to the 82d and 101st AbnDivs. The Canadians were reassigned to the 6th UK AbnDiv.

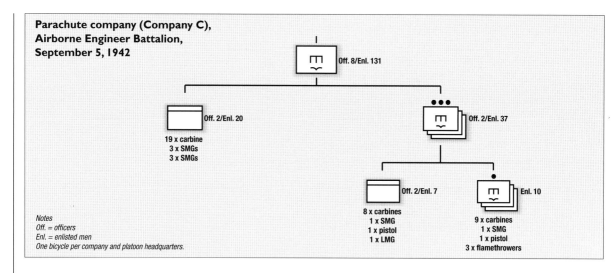

Parachute company (Company C), Airborne Engineer Battalion, September 5, 1942

Off. 8/Enl. 131

Off. 2/Enl. 20
19 x carbine
3 x SMGs
3 x SMGs

Off. 2/Enl. 37

Off. 2/Enl. 7
8 x carbines
1 x SMG
1 x pistol
1 x LMG

Enl. 10
9 x carbines
1 x SMG
1 x pistol
3 x flamethrowers

Notes
Off. = officers
Enl. = enlisted men
One bicycle per company and platoon headquarters.

PFAB with four 75mm howitzers as other batteries. The 503d Regimental Combat Team (RCT) took a different track with its Battery D, 462d PFAB reorganized into three platoons with four .50-cal. machine guns. A platoon would be attached to each battalion.

The 674th and 675th GFABs were organized differently to their parachute counterpart. Rather than three four-howitzer batteries, they had two six-tube 75mm howitzer batteries to support a glider regiment's two battalions. They also lacked the AA/AT battery. The 675th GFAB was rearmed with 105mm M3 howitzers in mid January 1945 on Leyte.

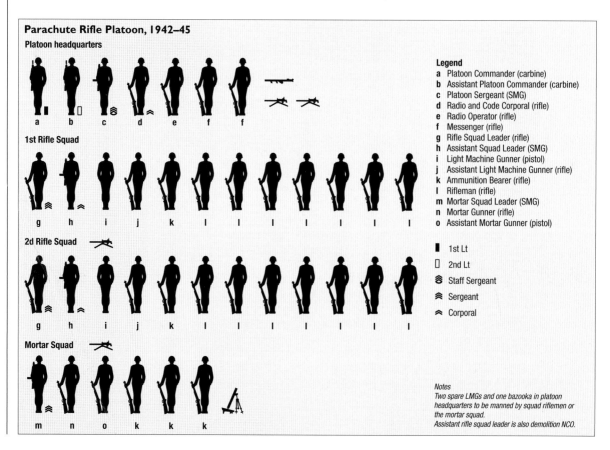

Parachute Rifle Platoon, 1942–45

Platoon headquarters

a   b   c   d   e   f   f

1st Rifle Squad

g   h   i   j   k   l   l   l   l   l   l

2d Rifle Squad

g   h   i   j   k   l   l   l   l   l   l

Mortar Squad

m   n   o   k   k   k

Legend
a   Platoon Commander (carbine)
b   Assistant Platoon Commander (carbine)
c   Platoon Sergeant (SMG)
d   Radio and Code Corporal (rifle)
e   Radio Operator (rifle)
f   Messenger (rifle)
g   Rifle Squad Leader (rifle)
h   Assistant Squad Leader (SMG)
i   Light Machine Gunner (pistol)
j   Assistant Light Machine Gunner (rifle)
k   Ammunition Bearer (rifle)
l   Rifleman (rifle)
m   Mortar Squad Leader (SMG)
n   Mortar Gunner (rifle)
o   Assistant Mortar Gunner (pistol)

■   1st Lt
▯   2nd Lt
❁   Staff Sergeant
⩘   Sergeant
⩘   Corporal

Notes
Two spare LMGs and one bazooka in platoon headquarters to be manned by squad riflemen or the mortar squad.
Assistant rifle squad leader is also demolition NCO.

Forcemen of the US/Canadian 1st Special Service Force on Kiska Island in the Aleutians in August 1943. The FSSF's 2d Regiment was prepared to make a reinforcing jump on to the island if necessary, but the Japanese had already evacuated Kiska 19 days earlier.

The airborne engineer battalion had a headquarters and headquarters company, medical detachment, two two-platoon glider companies, and a three-platoon parachute company (Company C). An engineer platoon would typically be attached to each infantry battalion, but could operate under regimental control. The engineer platoons were armed with light machine guns and bazookas, allowing them to fight as infantry.

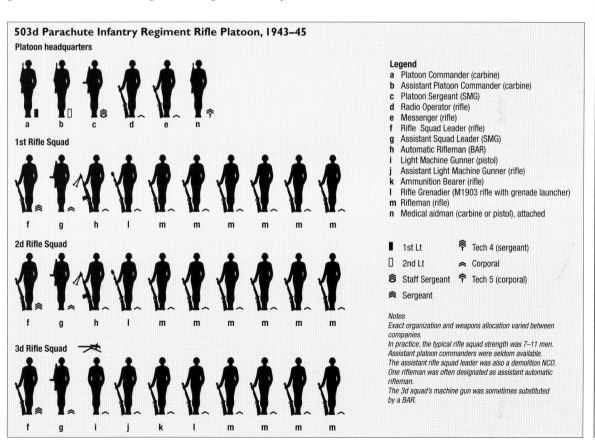

503d Parachute Infantry Regiment Rifle Platoon, 1943–45

Platoon headquarters

a, b, c, d, e, n

1st Rifle Squad

f, g, h, l, m, m, m, m, m, m

2d Rifle Squad

f, g, h, l, m, m, m, m, m, m

3d Rifle Squad

f, g, i, j, k, l, m, m, m, m

Legend
- **a** Platoon Commander (carbine)
- **b** Assistant Platoon Commander (carbine)
- **c** Platoon Sergeant (SMG)
- **d** Radio Operator (rifle)
- **e** Messenger (rifle)
- **f** Rifle Squad Leader (rifle)
- **g** Assistant Squad Leader (SMG)
- **h** Automatic Rifleman (BAR)
- **i** Light Machine Gunner (pistol)
- **j** Assistant Light Machine Gunner (rifle)
- **k** Ammunition Bearer (rifle)
- **l** Rifle Grenadier (M1903 rifle with grenade launcher)
- **m** Rifleman (rifle)
- **n** Medical aidman (carbine or pistol), attached

1st Lt		Tech 4 (sergeant)
2nd Lt		Corporal
Staff Sergeant		Tech 5 (corporal)
Sergeant		

Notes
Exact organization and weapons allocation varied between companies.
In practice, the typical rifle squad strength was 7–11 men.
Assistant platoon commanders were seldom available.
The assistant rifle squad leader was also a demolition NCO.
One rifleman was often designated as assistant automatic rifleman.
The 3d squad's machine gun was sometimes substituted by a BAR.

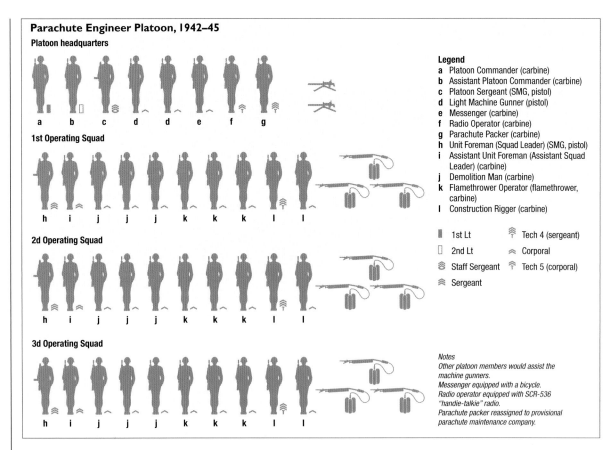

Parachute Engineer Platoon, 1942–45

Platoon headquarters

a b c d d e f g

Legend
a Platoon Commander (carbine)
b Assistant Platoon Commander (carbine)
c Platoon Sergeant (SMG, pistol)
d Light Machine Gunner (pistol)
e Messenger (carbine)
f Radio Operator (carbine)
g Parachute Packer (carbine)
h Unit Foreman (Squad Leader) (SMG, pistol)
i Assistant Unit Foreman (Assistant Squad Leader) (carbine)
j Demolition Man (carbine)
k Flamethrower Operator (flamethrower, carbine)
l Construction Rigger (carbine)

1st Operating Squad

h i j j j k k k l l

▌ 1st Lt   Tech 4 (sergeant)
▯ 2nd Lt   Corporal
Staff Sergeant   Tech 5 (corporal)
Sergeant

2d Operating Squad

h i j j j k k k l l

Notes
Other platoon members would assist the machine gunners.
Messenger equipped with a bicycle.
Radio operator equipped with SCR-536 "handie-talkie" radio.
Parachute packer reassigned to provisional parachute maintenance company.

3d Operating Squad

h i j j j k k k l l

Marine parachute units

When organized in 1941 and 1942, Marine parachute battalions were extremely light and intended for raiding and scouting. This was in observance with the Marine Corps policy of keeping specialized units, including the Raiders, small and compact, with the majority of troops assigned to the large and robust divisional infantry regiments. The parachute battalions were very lightly equipped, but well armed with automatic and other infantry weapons. They were provided minimal service support, organized into a rear detachment to link up on the ground after airlift or sealift landing. There were no medical personnel assigned to the headquarters company; they were in the rifle company headquarters.

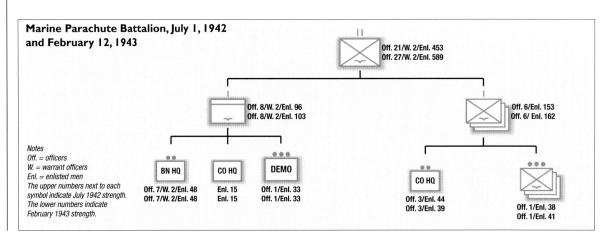

Marine Parachute Battalion, July 1, 1942 and February 12, 1943

Off. 21/W. 2/Enl. 453
Off. 27/W. 2/Enl. 589

Off. 8/W. 2/Enl. 96
Off. 8/W. 2/Enl. 103

Off. 6/Enl. 153
Off. 6/ Enl. 162

Notes
Off. = officers
W. = warrant officers
Enl. = enlisted men
The upper numbers next to each symbol indicate July 1942 strength. The lower numbers indicate February 1943 strength.

BN HQ
Off. 7/W. 2/Enl. 48
Off. 7/W. 2/Enl. 48

CO HQ
Enl. 15
Enl. 15

DEMO
Off. 1/Enl. 33
Off. 1/Enl. 33

CO HQ
Off. 3/Enl. 44
Off. 3/Enl. 39

Off. 1/Enl. 38
Off. 1/Enl. 41

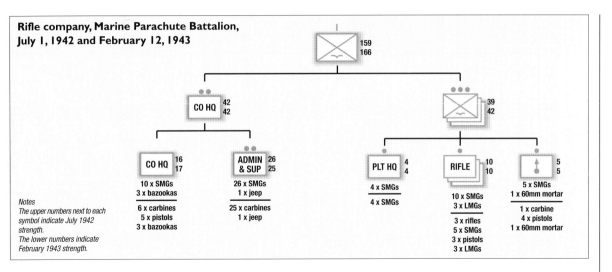

Rifle company, Marine Parachute Battalion, July 1, 1942 and February 12, 1943

159 / 166

CO HQ — 42 / 42

39 / 42

CO HQ — 16 / 17
- 10 x SMGs
- 3 x bazookas
- 6 x carbines
- 5 x pistols
- 3 x bazookas

ADMIN & SUP — 26 / 25
- 26 x SMGs
- 1 x jeep
- 25 x carbines
- 1 x jeep

PLT HQ — 4 / 4
- 4 x SMGs
- 4 x SMGs

RIFLE — 10 / 10
- 10 x SMGs
- 3 x LMGs
- 3 x rifles
- 5 x SMGs
- 3 x pistols
- 3 x LMGs

5 / 5
- 5 x SMGs
- 1 x 60mm mortar
- 1 x carbine
- 4 x pistols
- 1 x 60mm mortar

Notes
The upper numbers next to each symbol indicate July 1942 strength.
The lower numbers indicate February 1943 strength.

The parachute battalions went through four iterations. The first two T/Os did not see combat and will only be covered briefly. The battalions consisted of a headquarters company and three rifle companies, each with three rifle platoons and usually a weapons platoon. In most cases changes were minor with slight alterations in personnel and weapons. The same T/O number identified all battalions regardless of date: D-81 – parachute battalion, D-82 – headquarters company, and D-83 – rifle company.

In the tables that appear on pages 34–37, "O" indicates commissioned officers, "W" warrant officers, and "E" enlisted men. In the headquarters company and the rifle company headquarters two sets of strength figures are listed followed by a parenthesized (A) for the parachute-qualified air echelon and (G) for ground echelon, the rear echelon non-jumpers. The battalion strength included three surgeons and 15 hospital corpsmen with one surgeon and five corpsman per company headquarters, who were naval personnel. The companies were expected to conduct semi-independent missions.

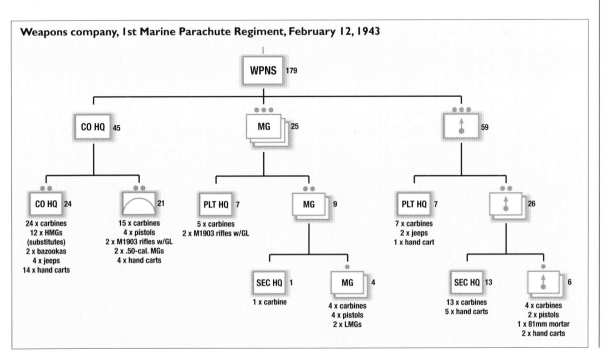

Weapons company, 1st Marine Parachute Regiment, February 12, 1943

WPNS — 179

CO HQ — 45

MG — 25

59

CO HQ — 24
- 24 x carbines
- 12 x HMGs (substitutes)
- 2 x bazookas
- 4 x jeeps
- 14 x hand carts

21
- 15 x carbines
- 4 x pistols
- 2 x M1903 rifles w/GL
- 2 x .50-cal. MGs
- 4 x hand carts

PLT HQ — 7
- 5 x carbines
- 2 x M1903 rifles w/GL

MG — 9

PLT HQ — 7
- 7 x carbines
- 2 x jeeps
- 1 x hand cart

26

SEC HQ — 1
- 1 x carbine

MG — 4
- 4 x carbines
- 4 x pistols
- 2 x LMGs

SEC HQ — 13
- 13 x carbines
- 5 x hand carts

6
- 4 x carbines
- 2 x pistols
- 1 x 81mm mortar
- 2 x hand carts

The March 28, 1941 battalion T/O was used by the 1st and 2d battalions. The machine-gun section had three M1919A4s and the mortar section three 60mm M2s. Vehicles included three 1½-ton and one ½-ton trucks and two motorcycles with sidecars in the administrative, maintenance, and supply section.

The 1st–3d Battalions were organized under the January 10, 1942 T/O. There were significant strength increases in the headquarters company and the rifle company headquarters as it was soon learned that additional support personnel were necessary. There were no changes in the rifle and weapons platoon personnel. The machine-gun section was supposed to have three "folding machine guns," but they retained M1919A4s. Assigned vehicles were three 2½-ton and one 1-ton trucks and three jeeps in the administrative,

Marine Parachute Battalion, March 28, 1941		
Parachute Battalion	O-24 E-448 (A) / O-5 W-1 E-75 (G)	
HQ Company	O-4 E-16 (A) / O-2 W-1 E-33 (G)	
Battalion HQ	O-4 E-2 (A) / O-2 E-3 (G)	
Intelligence Section	E-8 (A) / E-2 (G)	
Admin, Maint, & Supply Section	E-6 (A) / W-1 E-28 (G)	
Rifle Company (x 3)	O-6 E-144 (A) / O-1 E-14 (G)	
Company HQ Section	O-2 E-16 (A) / O-1 E-14 (G)	
	Company HQ	O-2 E-12
	Admin, Maint, & Supply Section	E-4 (A) / O-1 E-14 (G)
Rifle Platoon (x 3)	O-1 E-33	
	Platoon HQ	O-1 E-3
	Rifle Squad (x 3)	E-10
Weapons Platoon	O-1 E-29	
	Platoon HQ	O-1 E-3
	Machine-Gun Section	E-13
	Mortar Section	E-13

Marine parachute battalion, January 10, 1942		
Parachute Battalion	O-24 W-1 E-458 (A) / O-5 W-1 E-104 (G)	
HQ Company	O-6 W-1 E-20 (A) / O-2 W-1 E-41 (G)	
Battalion HQ	O-5 E-2 (A) / O-2 E-6 (G)	
Intelligence Section	E-8 (A) / E-2 (G)	
Admin, Maint, & Supply Section	W-1 E-10 (A) / W-1 E-33 (G)	
Rifle Company (x 3)	O-6 E-146 (A) / O-1 E-21 (G)	
Company HQ Section	O-2 E-18 (A) / O-1 E-21 (G)	
	Company HQ	O-2 E-13
	Admin, Maint, & Supply Section	E-5 (A) / O-1 E-21 (G)
Rifle Platoon (x 3)	O-1 E-33	
	Platoon HQ	O-1 E-3
	Rifle Squad (x 3)	E-10
Weapons Platoon	O-1 E-29	
	Platoon HQ	O-1 E-3
	Machine-Gun Section	E-13
	Mortar Section	E-13

maintenance, and supply section. The rifle company headquarters had a single jeep. Note that there was no headquarter company headquarters designated in the first two T/Os. The company commander was the battalion Bn-1/adjutant.

The 1st–3d Battalions were reorganized under the July 1, 1942 T/O. It was under this T/O that the 1st Battalion saw combat at Guadalcanal. Even more support personnel were added to the headquarters company and the company was internally reorganized to include the addition of a demolition platoon. It was organized as a rifle platoon, but with only two Johnson LMGs rather than three, and lacked the mortar squad. A headquarters company headquarters was added, but the commander was still the Bn-1/adjutant. The company weapons platoon was eliminated with three LMGs per rifle squad and a 60mm mortar squad in the rifle platoon. The nine light machine guns per rifle platoon were thought adequate to replace the M1919A4s in the weapons platoon. Assigning mortars to the rifle platoons may have been influenced by Army parachute unit practice, but the main goal was to eliminate the weapons platoon to reduce manpower. Vehicles were the same, except one jeep was deleted from the battalion headquarters.

The 1st–4th battalions were reorganized under the February 12, 1943 changes when the 1st Parachute Regiment was activated on April 1. The total ground echelon was now only one warrant officer and five enlisted men. There was no change in vehicle allocation.

Marine Parachute Battalion, July 1, 1942		
Parachute Battalion	O-21 W-1 E-453 (A) / O-5 W-1 E-102 (G)	
HQ Company	O-6 W-1 E-54 (A) / O-2 W-1 E-42 (G)	
Company HQ	E-15 (G)	
Battalion HQ Section	O-5 W-1 E-21 (A) / O-2 W-1 E-27 (G)	
Battalion HQ	O-5 E-2 (A) / O-2 E-5 (G)	
Communication Section	E-9	
Intelligence Section	E-8 (A) / E-2 (G)	
Maintenance & Supply Section	W-1 E-2 (A) / W-1 E-20 (G)	
Demolition Platoon	O-1 E-33	
Platoon HQ	O-1 E-3	
Demolition Squad (x 3)	E-10	
Rifle Company (x 3)	O-5 E-133 (A) / O-1 E-20 (G)	
Company HQ Section	O-2 E-19 (A) / O-1 E-20 (G)	
	Company HQ	O-2 E-14
	Admin & Supply Section	E-5 (A) / O-1 E-20 (G)
Rifle Platoon (x 3)	O-1 E-38	
	Platoon HQ	O-1 E-3
	Rifle Squad (x 3)	E-10
	Mortar Squad	E-5

When the 1st Parachute Regiment was activated a regimental headquarters company and a regimental weapons company were organized. Together with the increase in service personnel in the battalions, this made the parachute regiment a more sustainable unit. The regiment's authorized strength was 90 Marine officers, 11 warrant officers, and 2,071 enlisted men plus 16 Navy surgeons, medical officers, and 73 enlisted men.

The regimental weapons company provided 81mm mortars and heavy machine guns for the first time. The three machine-gun platoons were

(continued on page 38)

Marine Parachute Rifle Platoon, July 1, 1942

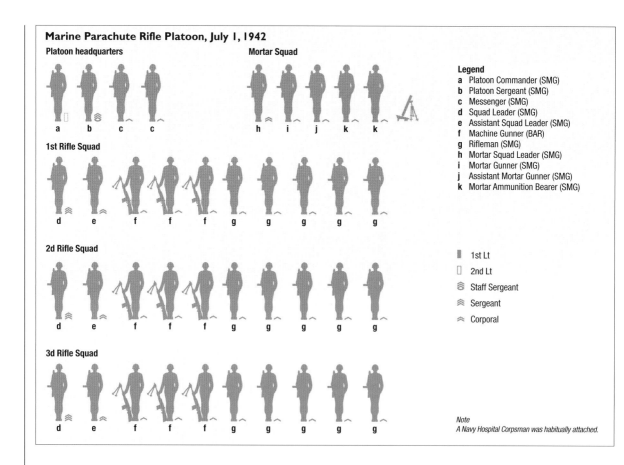

Platoon headquarters

a   b   c   c

Mortar Squad

h   i   j   k   k

1st Rifle Squad

d   e   f   f   f   g   g   g   g   g

2d Rifle Squad

d   e   f   f   f   g   g   g   g   g

3d Rifle Squad

d   e   f   f   f   g   g   g   g   g

Legend
- **a** Platoon Commander (SMG)
- **b** Platoon Sergeant (SMG)
- **c** Messenger (SMG)
- **d** Squad Leader (SMG)
- **e** Assistant Squad Leader (SMG)
- **f** Machine Gunner (BAR)
- **g** Rifleman (SMG)
- **h** Mortar Squad Leader (SMG)
- **i** Mortar Gunner (SMG)
- **j** Assistant Mortar Gunner (SMG)
- **k** Mortar Ammunition Bearer (SMG)

1st Lt

2nd Lt

Staff Sergeant

Sergeant

Corporal

Note
A Navy Hospital Corpsman was habitually attached.

Marine parachute battalion, February 12, 1943

Parachute Battalion	O-27 W-1 E-585 (A) / O-1 E-4 (G)
HQ Company	O-9 W-1 E-99 (A) / O-1 E-4 (G)
Company HQ	E-13 (A) / E-2 (G)
Battalion HQ Section	O-8 W-1 E-53 (A) / O-1 (G)
Battalion HQ	O-8 E-13
Communication Section	E-9
Intelligence Section	E-10
Maint & Supply Section	W-1 E-21 (A) / W-1 E-1 (G)
Demolition Platoon	O-1 E-33
Platoon HQ	O-1 E-3
Demolition Squad (x 3)	E-10
Rifle Company (x 3)	O-6 E-162
Company HQ Section	O-3 E-39
Company HQ	O-2 E-14
Admin & Supply Section	O-1 E-24
Rifle Platoon (x 3)	O-1 E-41
Platoon HQ	O-1 E-3
Rifle Squad (x 3)	E-11
Mortar Squad	E-5

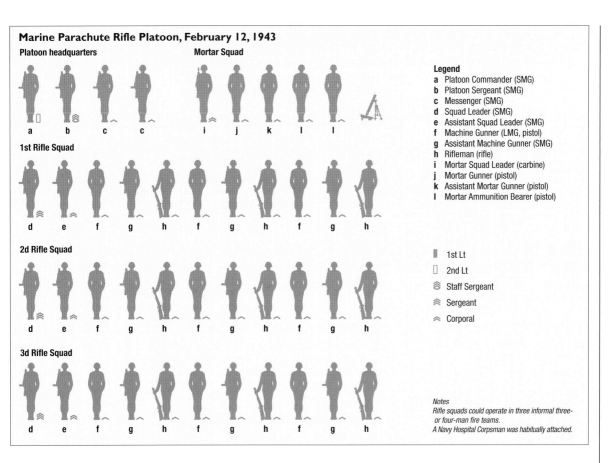

Marine Parachute Rifle Platoon, February 12, 1943

Platoon headquarters

a   b   c   c

Mortar Squad

i   j   k   l   l

1st Rifle Squad

d   e   f   g   h   f   g   h   f   g   h

2d Rifle Squad

d   e   f   g   h   f   g   h   f   g   h

3d Rifle Squad

d   e   f   g   h   f   g   h   f   g   h

Legend

- **a** Platoon Commander (SMG)
- **b** Platoon Sergeant (SMG)
- **c** Messenger (SMG)
- **d** Squad Leader (SMG)
- **e** Assistant Squad Leader (SMG)
- **f** Machine Gunner (LMG, pistol)
- **g** Assistant Machine Gunner (SMG)
- **h** Rifleman (rifle)
- **i** Mortar Squad Leader (carbine)
- **j** Mortar Gunner (pistol)
- **k** Assistant Mortar Gunner (pistol)
- **l** Mortar Ammunition Bearer (pistol)

   1st Lt

   2nd Lt

   Staff Sergeant

   Sergeant

   Corporal

Notes
*Rifle squads could operate in three informal three-
or four-man fire teams.*
A Navy Hospital Corpsman was habitually attached.

Marine Parachute Regiment Headquarters Company, April 1, 1943

Regimental HQ Company	O-13 W-2 E-108 (A) / O-3 W-1 E-54 (G)
Regimental HQ Section	O-7 E-21 (A) / O-3 E-9 (G)
Company HQ Section	E-26 (G)
Operations Section	O-2 E-5
Intelligence Section	O-2 E-15
Supply Section	E-1 (A) / W-1 E-19 (G)
Communication Platoon	O-1 E-39
Service Platoon	O-1 W-2 E-27

Marine Parachute Regiment Weapons Company, April 1, 1943

Regimental Weapons Company	O-7 E-172
Company HQ	O-3 E-42
Company HQ Section	O-2 E-21
Antiaircraft Section	E-21
Machine Gun Platoon (x 3)	O-1 E-24
Platoon HQ	O-1 E-6
MG Section (x 2)	E-9
Mortar Platoon	O-1 E-58
Platoon HQ	O-1 E-6
Mortar Section (x 2)	E-26

normally attached one per battalion. Each platoon had four M1919A4 LMGs organized into two two-squad sections (with one gun each). The company also had twelve M1917A1 watercooled HMGs as substitutes for long-range fire support and for defensive situations. The mortar platoon had four 81mm M1s. Assigned vehicles comprised four jeeps in the company headquarters and two in the mortar platoon headquarters.

Organic weapons, Marine Parachute Battalion

Weapon	March 1941	January 1942	July 1942	February 1943
.30-cal. M1 rifle[1]	—	—	—	81
.30-cal. M1903 rifle	243	—	—	8
.30-cal. M1/M1A1 carbine	—	—	—	232
.30-cal. M1918A2 BAR	18	12[2]	—	—
.30-cal. M1941 LMG	—	—	87[3]	87
.45-cal. M1928A1 SMG	72	—	—	135
.45-cal. M55 SMG	—	466	565	—
.45-cal. M1911A1 pistol	161	2	2	145
.30-cal. M1919A4 LMG	9	—	—	—
2.36in. M1 rocket launcher	—	—	9[4]	9
60mm M2 mortar	9	9	9	9
M1 grenade launcher	—	—	—	8

Notes
1. T/O called for Johnson M1941 rifles, but M1s were normally issued.
2. T/O called for a "folding machine gun." M1941 LMGs were not available and BARs were retained.
3. M1941 LMGs were not available. The M1919A4 was specified as a substitute, but it is believed BARs were used instead with one or two M1919A4s per platoon. Total includes six spares.
4. Bazookas unavailable in time for Guadalcanal.

Organic weapons, 1st Marine Parachute Regiment, 1943

Weapon	HQ & Service Co	Parachute Bn (x 3)	Weapons Co	Total
.30-cal. M1 rifle[1]	—	81	—	243
.30-cal. M1903 rifle	—	—	8	8
.30-cal. M1/M1A1 carbine	165	232	135	996
.30-cal. M1941 LMG	—	87[2]	—	261
.45-cal. M55/M1928A1 SMG	—	135	—	405
.45-cal. M1911A1 pistol	100[3]	145	36	571
.30-cal. M1919A4 LMG	—	—	12	12
.30-cal M1917A1 HMG	—	—	12[4]	12
.50-cal. M2 MG	—	—	2	2
2.36in. M1 rocket launcher	—	9	2	29
M1 flamethrower	9[3]	—	—	9
60mm M2 mortar	—	9	—	27
81mm M1 mortar	—	—	4	4
M1 grenade launcher	—	—	8	8

Notes
1. T/O called for Johnson M1941 rifles, but M1s were normally issued.
2. Includes six spares.
3. Weapons pooled in the HQ&S company's supply section.
4. Machine guns substituted for the LMGs.

Tactics

Airborne troops fought differently to ground-delivered infantry. Being inserted behind enemy lines, they could be surrounded, with attacks coming from any direction. There was no frontline with a rear area or supply and evacuation route in the normal sense. Supplies had to be delivered by airdrop, and this was at the mercy of the weather and enemy air activity. Service support units were small and lightly equipped.

Airborne troops lacked motorized transport to move weapons, ammunition, rations, water, and other supplies. The only way a small number of vehicles could be delivered to the airhead was by glider, and these were unavailable in the Pacific. This required everything to be moved by backpack or hand cart. It also severely limited the unit's offensive capabilities. Even with favorable weather conditions, there were still supply shortages due to damage caused to goods when dropped and the difficulty of moving supplies forward. Even when linked by a secure ground supply route, airborne units still had insufficient transport and support personnel.

While airborne units were provided a higher percentage of automatic weapons, they were still light in firepower. Heavier crew-served weapons were fewer in number and smaller in caliber than in equivalent conventional units, and the substitute weapons also had shorter ranges.

Regimental weapons comparison, 1943–45				
Weapon	Parachute	Glider	Marine	Standard
.30-cal. M1/M1903 rifle	1,173	792	251	1,990
.30-cal. M1/M1A1 carbine	495	635	996	843
.45-cal. M1928A1 SMG	154	—	405	—
.30-cal. M1918A2 BAR	—	42	261 (M1941)	81
.30-cal. M1919A4 LMG	132	20	12	18
.30-cal. M1917A1 HMG	—	—	12 (substitutes) 24	
37mm M3A1 AT gun	—	8	—	18
2.36in. M1/M1A1 rocket launcher	73	72	29	112
60mm M2 mortar	27	24	27	18
81mm M1 mortar	12	12	4	18

Units were lighter in strength and reduced not only the frontage they could occupy, but also the amount of time they could remain effective when suffering high losses. Additional automatic weapons only partly made up for fewer riflemen.

The insertion of an airborne unit resulted in immediate casualties even before enemy contact was made. The injuries were actually not all that high when compared to the casualties suffered in an amphibious assault. While there were fractures, most injuries were minor and those afflicted soon returned to action. Sufficient medical support had to be dropped in with the assault as casualties could only be evacuated by air, and it might be sometime before an airstrip could be readied. Under the best of circumstances it required at least an hour for a battalion to assemble, but it could sometimes take up to five hours. It was critical that the location of the DZ was wisely selected in relation to enemy positions.

A major factor affecting tactics was unit structure. Parachute rifle platoons had only two rifle squads. The glider regiment had only two battalions, and a glider company had only two rifle platoons. It thus had no reserve battalion to reinforce or exploit success, provide depth to the defense, and rotate battalions to allow one a degree of rest in order to maintain tempo. It was also difficult for a two-battalion regiment to relieve a three-battalion regiment and accomplish the same mission.

Regimental organization comparison, 1942–44				
Subunit	**Parachute**	**Glider**	**Marine**	**Standard**
Battalions	3	2	4	3
Rifle companies	9	6	12	9
Rifle platoons	27	12	36	27
Rifle squads	54	36	108	81
Trucks, all types	39	26	39	214
Total strength	1,958	1,678	2,022	3,087

Gen Swing handled this problem differently to his European counterparts, a "luxury" afforded to him by the nature of the terrain and the tactical situations his division faced. On both Leyte and Luzon the division was fighting on a narrow front and was connected by extremely long supply lines to its beachhead. Its familiarity with airborne operations complemented its aerial resupply. Swing recognized the inadequacy of two-battalion regiments. He compensated for this by only employing two regiments in direct combat. Units were of course rotated to some degree, but typically the 511th PIR with its three battalions was committed along with one of the glider regiments reinforced by a battalion from its sister regiment. The "one-battalion regiment" was responsible for rear security and maintaining the supply line along with the antiaircraft and engineer battalions, and service units. The division seldom had a reserve of any kind unless it was an attached unit.

On Leyte there was little need, or rather little opportunity, to use artillery. The mud track leading into the mountains precluded its advance. A single 75mm battery was airdropped into a forward position though, and longer-ranged, non-divisional artillery provided support. The division's two glider artillery battalions were reorganized as infantry, augmenting their armament with Japanese machine guns and 5cm grenade dischargers ("knee mortars"); they too provided rear security. To augment the division's short-ranged 75mm and 105mm pack howitzers, standard 105mm and 155mm howitzer battalions were attached for much of its service. Rear security was essential owing to infiltrators, Japanese attempts to deliver raiders by parachute or crash-landing transports, and for defending against counterlandings on the beachhead.

On Luzon especially, additional infantry battalions and even regiments were attached to the 11th to augment its capabilities during the fighting on the approaches to Manila and in southern Luzon. Tank, tank destroyer, and self-propelled howitzer companies were also attached and good use was made of these armor-protected and mobile assault guns.

Another form of rear-area security was the defense of the drop area once a unit parachuted in. A battalion was usually assigned this task. It mopped up the area, and secured the dropped-in artillery position, command post, aid station, and supply points. It also assisted with recovering airdrop bundles and clearing an airstrip or any obstacles from an existing airfield.

Infantry tactics were straightforward. Most of the fighting experienced by airborne units was on hilly terrain covered by dense vegetation. The Japanese deployed their defensive positions in mutually supporting belts and in depth. To attack one position meant receiving fire from others. Visibility was limited and land navigation difficult. This affected the ability to call for and adjust artillery and mortar fire. Fighting in this environment was largely borne by small units, at platoon level and below. Five- to six-man teams assaulted pillboxes using grenades, bazookas, flamethowers, and demolitions. They were covered by small arms, machine guns, and mortars. Small reconnaissance and combat patrols were constant. During the day the infantry fought their way forward and patrolled. At night they took up and maintained tight defensive positions; no movement was permitted inside friendly lines during the hours of darkness.

The antiaircraft battalion seldom operated in its intended role. Its antitank guns were detached to infantry regiments for direct fire support against pillboxes and fortified buildings, in those areas where the terrain permitted them to be manhandled. The .50-cal. machine guns were also attached to the infantry for direct fire against ground targets. While heavy to manhandle, they were ideal for cutting through dense vegetation and shooting up field fortifications. They also provided valuable long-range support, as parachute units lacked .30-cal. watercooled heavy machine guns.

A major difference between PTO airborne operations and those in the Mediterranean and Europe was that all were conducted in daylight. While units occasionally missed DZs, they were still dropped close together. This greatly decreased assembly time.

Weapons and equipment

With regard to the overall size of the Army and Marine Corps, airborne units made up a small percentage of their forces. As desirable as it may have been to develop lighter and more compact weapons for the airborne, it was not cost effective, and would burden production lines and complicate the spare parts system. For this reason standard weapons were used to the maximum extent or were slightly modified for the needs of the airborne. A few weapons were developed later to meet airborne requirements, but they would also be used by conventional units, as compactness was equally valuable to them.

It was of course highly desirable for paratroopers to jump with their individual weapons, so that they might be ready immediately for action on the ground. This was difficult to do with M1903 and M1 rifles and BARs. The use of drop containers with a squad's individual weapons loaded was not ideal, as there were instances when paratroopers were unable to locate their containers and had to continue the attack with their pistols. There was a danger too of the containers falling into enemy hands. Both the Japanese and Germans experienced these problems. Locating containers was also extremely difficult at night and among vegetation. This was even more problematic in the dense vegetation on many of the Pacific drop zones.

Some American individual weapons could be broken down and carried in small canvas containers attached to the jumper. Other weapons were compact enough to be strapped to the jumper's parachute harness. The 503d PIR actually jumped with their weapons in their hands, but still attached to them in case they had to use their hands to deploy their reserve parachute or steer away from obstacles. Glider troops for the most part used standard weapons, including some of the heavier crew-served weapons denied to paratroopers.

Army weapons

The Army employed the .30-cal. M1 Garand rifle; .30-cal. M1903, M1903A1, and M1903A3 Springfield rifles (mainly for grenade launching); .30-cal. M1 and M1A1 carbines; .45-cal. M1928A1, M1, and M1A1 Thompson submachine guns (SMGs); .45-cal. M1911 and M1911A1 Colt pistols; and .30-cal. M1918A2 BARs.[8]

A disadvantage of the carbine was that it sounded like the Japanese 6.5mm rifle, and could thus draw friendly fire. Another carbine version was the M1A3 issued in late 1944. This had a pantographic metal stock folding under the weapon, which was lighter and stronger then the M1A1's side-folding stock. It was 25.5in. long with the stock folded and weighed 5.5lb. It was to replace the M1A1, but the war's end saw the halt of its production and few were issued. The 503d PIR used the M1A3 on Corregidor.

While carbines were widely used, they made for a poor frontline combat weapon, and instead infantrymen relied on the semi-automatic M1 rifle. An M1-armed soldier could fire off 15–18 aimed shots per minute compared to an Arisaka-armed Japanese soldier's 8–10 rounds. The M1903A4 Springfield sniper rifle saw some use, but the telescoped rifles were withdrawn from the 503d PIR, probably because their long range was found unnecessary in the jungle.

Thompson SMGs saw only limited use. They were heavy, difficult to maintain, had poor penetration through dense brush and bamboo, and sounded like Japanese LMGs. The .45-cal M3 SMG (or "grease gun") was issued

A 503d PIR BAR man fires rounds into a Japanese position on Corregidor, February 20, 1945. The 19.4lb., .30-cal. M1918A2 BAR was not assigned to the parachute rifle squads, but both the 503d and 511th PIRs issued them in lieu of the .30-cal. M1919A4 LMG owing to the latter's weight issues.

---

8 A fuller treatment of individual weapons characteristics is provided in Battle Orders 22: *US Airborne Units in the Mediterranean Theater 1942–44*.

late in the war and saw some use. Initially it was unpopular, but the men soon learned it was a rugged, reliable weapon. The M1918A2 BAR was considered too bulky for jumping and was not issued to parachute units, but was issued to glider troops. The 503d and 511th PIR both used it though, it being lighter than the M1919A4 LMG.

The M1903 rifle used the M1 grenade launcher until the M7 was available for the M1 rifle in late 1943. These launched M9A1 antitank, M17 antipersonnel, and various pyrotechnic signal (colored smoke and flare) grenades. There were also tailboom adapters, which allowed fragmentation or smoke hand grenades to be attached and fired as rifle grenades.

The Mk II and Mk IIA1 "pineapple" fragmentation were the standard anti-personnel grenades. The Mk IIIA1 demolition or "concussion" grenade was an offensive grenade heavy on blast, but generating only secondary fragmentation (rock and wood splinters). The AN-M8 white smoke grenade was used for screening and target marking. The AN-M14 incendiary grenade was used for destroying enemy equipment. Its termite filler burnt through steel at 4,330°F (2,387°C). The M15 white phosphorus was a bursting-type casualty-producing grenade. It threw out particles of 5,000°F (2,760°C) phosphorus and was ideal for clearing pillboxes and attacking troops in open-topped positions. It was also used for instant smoke screening. The M16 and M18 colored smoke grenades were used for ground-to-ground and air-to-ground signaling. The M16 was available in red, yellow, green, violet, orange, blue, and black. The M18, which burned more vividly and longer, was available in only the first four colors.

The .30-cal. M1919A4 Browning LMG provided the parachute rifle platoon with significant firepower. Although they were intended to be dropped in separate containers, there were instances where they were carried by paratroopers. The M1919A6 was introduced in late 1944, but appears to have seen limited use in the PTO.

A valuable weapon was the 2.36in. shoulder-fired bazooka antitank rocket launcher. Parachute infantry units were not authorized bazookas in the original September 1942 T/O, but their issue was authorized in December. The 503d PIR did not receive bazookas until late 1944. Although no airborne unit in the PTO faced tanks, they were very useful for attacking pillboxes and defended buildings. The M1 bazooka (two handgrips) was introduced in 1942 and the M1A1 (one handgrip) in 1943. Paratroopers developed a tube-like canvas drop bag for the bulky weapon that was lowered on a rope once the parachute opened. This was an awkward arrangement and the Airborne Command requested a two-piece bazooka that could be broken down into two sections for jumping and ground transport. This had the advantage of allowing for a longer tube to increase range. The M9 and M9A1 (improved barrel coupling latch) were issued to airborne units in late 1944.

Parachute engineer companies had 27 M1 or M1A1 portable flamethrowers, and from June 1942 the parachute regiment headquarters company had 12 for use by rifle companies. These proved to be extremely useful against pillboxes and fortified buildings, especially in Manila.

Owing to the limited armor threat in the Pacific airborne units did not receive bazookas until late 1944. Here a member of Company C, 161st Engineer Battalion fires a 2.36in. M9 bazooka at a pillbox on Corregidor. Slung on his back is a .30-cal. M1A3 pantographic folding stock.

Flamethrowers were rarely used by the airborne, although they could be dropped by parachute. They were widely used when cracking the Genko Line outside Manila and on Corregidor. This is the later model M2-2, which replaced the shorter-ranged and less effective M1 and M1A1.

Marine weapons

Marine parachute units mostly used the same weapons as their Army counterparts, including the .30-cal. M1 rifle from 1943, .30-cal. M1903-series rifles (mainly used for grenade launching), .30-cal. M1A1 and some M1 carbines, .30-cal. M1918A2 BARs, .45-cal. M1928A1 SMGs, .45-cal. M1911A1 pistol, and M1 rifle grenade launcher for the M1903 rifle. Heavier weapons included the .30-cal. M1919A4 LMG, 60mm M2 mortar, and 2.36in. M1 bazookas. The bazookas were not received until late 1943.

Three weapons unique to the Marines were also employed. While all of these weapons possessed innovative features and offered some benefits, they were overall found wanting, and withdrawn in 1943.

One of the worst weapons ever used by the US armed forces was the Reising SMG. The .45-cal. M50 and M55 Reising were introduced in 1942 because Thompson SMG production was being diverted to the British and the US Army. The Reising would also serve as a substitute for the M1 carbine, which was also being diverted to the Army. The M50 had a solid wooden stock and the M55 a flimsy folding wire stock, a pistol grip, and it lacked a muzzle compensator. The M55 weighed 6.25 lb. and was 31.25in. long with the stock extended and 22.5in. with it folded. It had a 20-round magazine. It was issued to parachute battalions, who initially were armed with 656 Reisings and no rifles. These were largely replaced by rifles and carbines, but Reisings saw action early on. Reising guns proved to be prone to jamming, especially in sandy conditions, and rusting. This was not because of the design, but because poor-quality metals were used and because rapid production had reduced the weapons' tolerances. In late 1943 the "Rusting Gun" was withdrawn.

Paratroopers used a small number of .30-cal. M1941 Johnson rifles, a semi-automatic with a ten-round magazine. Developed by a Marine Reserve officer, the Johnson had some advantages over the M1 rifle. It was the same weight as an M1, 9.5 lb., had a ten-round rotary (as opposed to an eight-round) magazine, and could be loaded using M1903 Springfield five-round stripper clips. It could be loaded with single rounds to fill up the magazine; this could not be done with the M1. However, the weapon was not as rugged as the M1 rifle. It had a recoiling barrel, prone to jamming in sand, and its numerous small parts were easily lost during field stripping. Because of the recoiling barrel it could only handle a very light, short bayonet, which lacked a grip, preventing it from being used as a knife. The recoiling barrel could not deal with the recoil of a grenade launcher, but it could be removed to shorten the weapon for a container jump. Efforts were made to standardize the Johnson and even for the Army to adopt it, but the M1 rifle was here to stay. Only 23 Johnsons were known to have been used in combat on Gavutu-Tanambogo and Guadalcanal by the 1st Parachute Battalion, one per squad. Johnsons were used in combat by later battalions.

Marine paratroopers initially used the .45-cal. Reising M55 folding stock submachine gun as their basic weapon. However, it was soon replaced by Thompson submachine guns, M1 carbines, and M1 rifles.

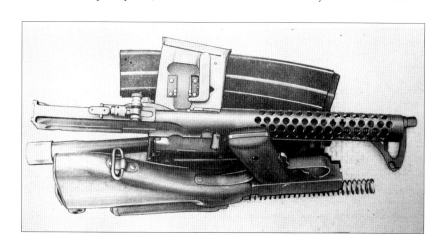

The .30-cal. M1941 Johnson light machine gun disassembled and ready to pack into a small pack for parachute dumping. The "Johnny gun" was used by both Marine paratroopers and the 1st Special Service Force in lieu of the BAR. (USN)

Another Johnson weapon was the .30-cal. M1941 LMG with a 20-round, side-feed magazine and bipod. The M1941 was issued as a squad automatic weapon in lieu of the BAR, and was sometimes described as an automatic rifle disguised as a light machine gun. The "Johnny gun" was lighter than the BAR at 14 lb. and the barrel could be removed and broken down into three components to allow it to be easily packed in a jump container. It could be reassembled in under a minute, and its rate of fire was 400–450 rpm. A quantity of Johnson rifles and machine guns was ordered by the Netherlands East Indies Army. A few were delivered before the war, but the bulk of the order was impounded after Pearl Harbor and turned over to the Marines. Both Johnsons were withdrawn from use in 1943, mainly because it was more efficient to produce only one rifle and one squad automatic weapon common to all the armed forces. The FSSF obtained 125 M1941 LMGs from the Marines (in time for the August 1943 Kiska landing) and used them in lieu of BARs into 1944.

The .30-cal. Johnson M1941 LMG was 6.4 lb. lighter than the BAR, but it was not as rugged a weapon and was withdrawn in 1943. The FSSF used "Johnny guns" into 1944 though.

Crew-served weapons

The 60mm M2 mortar was provided to rifle platoons while the 81mm M1 was a battalion weapon. They were broken down into two and three man-packed loads, but were dropped in a single container. The 503d PIR made limited use of an experimental 60mm, tripod-mounted, direct-fire mortar fitted with a shoulder pad, possibly the T21. Both calibers of mortar were provided HE, WP, and illumination rounds. Illumination for both mortars was not made available until 1944; WP was available in 1943 for the 81mm and 1944 for the 60mm.

Parachute and glider units were issued the 37mm M3A1 antitank gun. This weapon was in theory air-droppable using several cargo parachutes and slung beneath a transport. In so far as is known, this was never done in the PTO nor were they landed by glider with its ten-man crew. By 1941 the 37mm was obsolete and in the European Theater it began to be replaced by the 57mm M1 AT gun in 1943. Some standard infantry units in the Pacific received the 57mm, although it never entirely replaced its smaller brother and the airborne retained the "thirty-seven." The 37mm remained effective against Japanese tanks, a threat which the 11th AbnDiv never faced. It was provided with armor piercing, high-explosive, and canister rounds, which were effective against pillboxes and buildings. The canister round was used to strip camouflaging vegetation from pillboxes. This gun was towed by a 1/4-ton jeep.

Each parachute rifle platoon was assigned a 42lb. 60mm M2 mortar – three per company. The glider rifle platoon also had a 60mm mortar in its two rifle platoons, plus two more in the company weapons platoon.

The primary field artillery piece for both parachute and glider field artillery battalions was the 75mm M1A1 pack howitzer. A jeep served as its main prime mover, and it could be relatively easily manhandled about the battlefield by its 12-man crew. Besides the prime mover, each howitzer was provided a second jeep with a ¼-ton trailer for ammunition. When the pieces had to be manhandled forward, the M4 cart pulled by two men was available. It could only carry ten rounds though. This "seventy-five pack" could be disassembled and airdropped in seven types of specially designed

Parachute and glider infantry battalion mortar platoons had four and six, respectively, 136lb. 81mm M1 mortars. Both the 60mm and 81mm mortars could be dropped in a single parachute container. Ammunition was dropped in separate containers.

The 75mm M1A1 pack howitzer was broken down into nine loads for para-drop. This is the M1 paracrate, tipped on its side, for holding the front trail assembly. Usually it was tightly wrapped in canvas for protection from mud. It was dropped using a 48ft-diameter cargo parachute.

A Marine R4D, basically the same as the Army Air Forces C-47, drops paratroopers in a practice jump. The C-47 was the workhorse of the airborne, dropping paratroopers in all operations. Only a few larger C-46s were employed for the Camalaniugan operation, the war's last combat jump.

"paracrates" intended for specific components for nine bundles. Special "parachests" and a steel-wheeled "paracaisson" were used to drop ammunition. Six bundles were rigged on underwing and underbelly bomb shackles, and three loads were flung out the door. The bundles were connected by web straps to keep them together, easing recovery.

The 105mm M3 howitzer was standardized in February 1942 and was a shortened, standard M2A1 howitzer barrel mounted on a lightweight carriage. The 2,495 lb. weapon could not be airdropped, and was carried in gliders and transports. The "snub-nose" 105's range was 8,295 yds, about 1,500 yds shorter than the 75mm pack and only about two-thirds the range of the 105mm M2A1.

Antiaircraft weapons were originally thought to be critical, as it was expected for paratroopers to be vulnerable to air attack, but in reality there was little need for them. AA battalions were armed with 84 lb., .50-cal. M2 Browning machine guns on 375 lb. M2A1 AA mounts. The "fifty-cal" could also be fired from 44 lb. M3 ground tripods.

The airlift

The Douglas C-47A Skytrain or "Gooney Bird" transport was the primary troop carrier, parachute jump, and glider tug used by the US Army Air Forces (USAAF). This was a twin-engine aircraft based on the commercial DC-3. It had up to a 1,500-mile range and could lift 6,000 lb. of cargo, or 28 combat-loaded soldiers, or 18 litters. Typically 15–19 jumpers were carried. A 37mm antitank gun, 105mm M3, 75mm M1A1 howitzer, or a ¼-ton jeep could be carried. It was not designed with the jeep in mind, but it fortunately turned out that one could be loaded through the left side cargo door – also the jump exit door. Six large drop bundles could also be carried beneath the wings and fuselage. The Navy and Marine Corps used it as the R4D.

A parachute infantry regiment required 117 C-47s, and this was without attachments. A battalion required 36 and a rifle company nine. A parachute field artillery battalion required fifty-two C-47s, and a battery 12, as did a parachute engineer company.

Re-supply drops for parachute units were essential, and the standard cargo parachute was the 24ft G-1 made of colored cotton. The color identified the cargo: red for ammunition and demolitions, blue for water, yellow for rations, white for medical supplies, and green for other supplies. Water was dropped in bundles of 5-gal cans, which often failed to survive the experience.

Command, control, communications, and intelligence

One of the main principles learned about the command and control of airborne units was that they had to be held under the control of the theater of operations, or at the least that of a subordinate field army. This ensured they were employed for essential missions, and not used for some trivial role or as just another ground unit, which of course sometimes had to be the case. It also required a higher headquarters to ensure effective coordination with the USAAF and adequate logistical support. The higher headquarters would ensure that the airborne unit was effectively integrated into the ground force's plans. Upon air-delivery and the subsequent link up with the ground force, the airborne unit would come under the control of the major ground commander, no lower than corps level.

11th AbnDiv command assignments	
Airborne Command	25 February 1943
XXI Corps	2 January 1944
Sixth Army	25 May 1944
X Corps	24 August 1944
Sixth Army	28 September 1944
Eighth Army	26 Decemeber 1944
Sixth Army	9 February 1945
XIV Corps	10 February 1945
Sixth Army	15 June 1945
Eighth Army	15 August 1945

With the arrival of the 11th AbnDiv, Maj Gen Swing attempted to have the 503d PRCT assigned to the division. Macarthur wisely kept it separate, preserving it for special missions.

Army airborne unit staff organization has been discussed in Battle Orders 22, and so only a brief discussion of Marine staff organization is provided here. The Marines did not use "S" to identify staff officers/sections, but rather "Bn" and "R" to identify the staff officer's echelon. The parachute battalion staff was small; the commander was a lieutenant colonel, often a major in practice, and there was a major executive officer, captains as the Bn-3 (operations) and Bn-4 (supply), and two lieutenants as the Bn-2 (intelligence) and Bn-1 (adjutant/personnel) who doubled as the headquarters company CO. The regimental staff had a colonel CO, lieutenant colonel XO, major R-3 (operations), three captains as the R-1 (adjutant), R-2 (intelligence), and R-4 (supply), and three lieutenants as the assistant R-1 (headquarters company commander), assistant R-3, and assistant R-4 (munitions officer). Company COs were captains, except for the weapons company (commanded by a major).

Communications were of course critical for an airborne unit. When dropped in, the units sometimes became scattered and radios aided their assembly. Radios of the era, though, were heavy, temperamental, fragile, short ranged, and used batteries at a high rate or were powered by heavy, hand-cranked generators. The short range of tactical radios was a real problem in hilly jungle areas, and units often could not reach higher headquarters or adjacent units.

Maj Gen Joseph M. Swing greets Gen Walther Kruger, Commanding Sixth Army, as he visits the 11th AbnDiv prior to the June 1945 Camalaniugan operation, the last combat jump of World War II.

A technique used on Leyte was called the "Mosely Milk Run," named after a member of the 11th AbnDiv's G-3 Section. He would go airborne in an L-4 each day at 0730 and 1630, overflying each unit in the hills and making radio contact to receive reports and requests, drop messages, discuss the situation with commanders, and plot unit positions. The division published a newspaper, the *Static Line*, and dropped it to forward units.

Field telephones proved ineffective in the hills and there was insufficient wire. The Japanese constantly cut lines, meaning there were long periods without communications. A great deal of time and manpower were required to repair the lines, and the Japanese sometimes ambushed repair parties. Since radios were so short ranged, the 152d AA Battalion established the "Godfrey Relay" to maintain radio contact between forward units and the rear command posts and support units. Small radio teams with a few security personnel moved into the hills setting up SCR-609 radios in advantageous sites along the access trails. Godfrey 12 was at Manarawat, the forward support base. As units advanced, additional stations were established. The system proved essential to the Leyte operation's success.

Intelligence of the area of operations, especially of the DZ and the surrounding area, was essential. This was usually acquired from aerial photographs. This, however, had its limitations owing to the dense jungle. Even low kauri grass concealed obstacles and flooded areas. Maps were more often than not inaccurate, if available at all. Airborne divisions and their subordinate units possessed no organic reconnaissance subunits, such as the company-size divisional reconnaissance troop or regimental intelligence and reconnaissance platoons. Scouting and patrolling were undertaken by rifle companies. The 11th, though, like all airborne divisions, formed a provisional reconnaissance platoon to perform essential missions. Regimental demolition platoons were also sometimes used for this purpose.

Combat operations

Marine parachute units in the Solomons

While the Marine parachute battalions did not conduct any airborne operations, they did fight as light infantry, conducted raids and diversionary operations, and participated in amphibious assaults. The first amphibious landing and offensive ground operation conducted by the US in World War II featured the 1st Parachute Battalion.

The 1st MarDiv was tasked to land on Guadalcanal on August 7, 1942 to seize an airfield under construction by the Japanese. Operation *Watchtower* comprised near simultaneous landings on Guadalcanal and smaller islands 23 miles north-northeast across The Slot and just off the south-central coast of Florida Island. These included Tulagi (site of the Japanese headquarters), and smaller Gavatu and Tanambogo connected by a 300 yard-long causeway. Some 3,000 Japanese construction, air service, and Special Naval Landing Force (SNLF) troops were working on the airfield. SNLF and communications detachments were also present on Tulagi (350) and Gavatu-Tanambogo (550).

The 1st MarDiv had just over 19,000 personnel, but was barely adequate for the mission. The multiple, simultaneous objectives plus the need to maintain a reserve meant there were too few battalions. Two Marine regiments with five battalions would land on Guadalcanal to take the airfield. One regiment (less elements) was held in reserve and the parachute, raider, and two infantry battalions would seize the smaller islands – the 3,900-man Northern Group under the assistant division commander. The use of the paratroopers and raiders as first-wave assault troops was not how they were envisioned for deployment. While possessing substantial automatic firepower, they were lacking in heavier weapons and were not nearly as strong as infantry battalions. Rather than attacking at three-to-one odds, the 361 paratroopers were outnumbered by the Gavatu-Tanambogo defenders by at least 200. Gavatu is only 250 x 500 yards and Tanambogo just 250 yards across, topped, respectively, by 148ft-high and 175ft-high central coral hills. These were honeycombed with caves and covered by dense brush and trees. The battalion

Marine paratroopers on Cape Torokina, Bougainville. Both the camouflage jungle uniform and jump suits were made from much too heavy a fabric, and proved to be far too hot as well as taking too long to dry out. The third man to the right is armed with a .30-cal. Springfield M1903 rifle. Mk II fragmentation hand grenades can be seen hanging on the web gear.

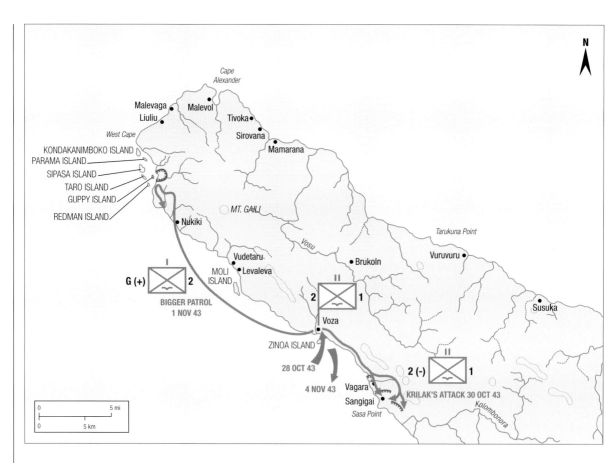

The Choiseul diversion, 2d Parachute Battalion, October 28–November 4, 1943.

rear echelon had been left in New Zealand. Company C had only two platoons. While well trained, it was less than proficient at amphibious landings.

The first landing was conducted by 1/2 Marines at H-20 minutes (0740 hours); they searched points on Florida's south coast, but found no enemy troops. The 1st Raider Battalion landed against strong opposition on Tulagi at H-Hour (0800 hours) followed by 2/5 Marines at 0916 hours. The 1st Parachute Battalion, as the Gavutu Group, was to land on Gavutu's northeast side at H+4 hours (1200).

The islands had been heavily hammered by naval 5in. guns and dive-bombed. The shell damage to the seaplane ramp forced the paratroopers of Company A to land on a small beach and pier. They made it ashore experiencing only light fire. Four minutes later when Company B landed, the enemy had recovered and inflicted casualties, as it did on Company C following three minutes later. Company A only advanced 75 yards before it was halted. Company C took up positions to fire on Tanambogo, from where punishing fire was being directed against the Marines *en enfilade*. The paratroopers were unprepared to deal with cave defenses, and had to learn how to defeat them the hard way. Casualties mounted, and Maj Robert H. Williams was wounded 20 minutes after landing; the XO, Maj Charles A. Miller, took over. By 1430 hours the eastern half of the island was secure, but the fire from Tanambogo kept the Marines from clearing the western portion. After US destroyers and dive-bombers had worked over Tanambogo, Gavutu was secured at 1800 hours. Reinforced by Company B, 1/2 Marines, the attack on Tanambogo commenced in the evening, with the rifle company attempting an amphibious landing on the island's north side while the paratroopers assaulted across the causeway. The attack was driven off and the island was not taken until the next day by 3/2 Marines.

The 1st Parachute Battalion had lost 28 killed in action (KIA) and 50 wounded in action (WIA) including key officers and NCOs. The 1st Raider Battalion on Tulagi had suffered only 10 percent casualties. On August 9, the battalion was moved to larger Tulagi and took up defensive positions. The Reising submachine guns were found wanting and many paratroopers rearmed themselves with Springfield rifles collected from other units' casualties. At the beginning of September the 1st Parachute Battalion was brought over to the Henderson Field Perimeter and placed in reserve. There many paratroopers were taken ill, and the battalion's effective strength dwindled. As so many of its leaders were casualties or ill, including the acting commander, the battalion was attached to the 1st Raider Battalion on September 3 to become the Raider-Parachute Battalion under the Raider battalion commander, Lt Col Merritt A. Edson. The Raider and parachute companies retained their identities, though.

The Japanese navy was landing reinforcements and supplies at points on both sides of the Marine perimeter. To keep the enemy off balance, the battalion executed an amphibious harassing raid 18 miles east of the perimeter at Tasimboko on September 8. The Raiders landed east of the enemy position at dawn; soon contact was made, and the fighting intensified. The 208 paratroopers (less Company C) came ashore at 1130 hours and went into defensive positions to the Raiders' left. An enveloping landing to the west was requested, but 1st MarDiv could not reduce the overextended units defending the perimeter and recommended that the force withdraw. They continued to fight on against a rearguard, but it withdrew and the Marines gained the village and destroyed supplies and equipment. The force was extracted that afternoon losing two KIA and six WIA.

On September 10 the Raider-Parachute Battalion[9] dug in on a grass-covered ridge on the south-central portion of the perimeter, with the Raiders on the west side and the paratroopers on the east. Evidence found at Tasimboko and other intelligence indicated the Japanese would launch an attack on the perimeter. Surrounded by dense jungle and running perpendicular to the perimeter, the ridge pointed toward Henderson Field and might have been a main Japanese attack route. Most Marine units were defending the perimeter's flanks and its beaches against counterlandings. The inland perimeter was only thinly outposted.

The 2,500-man Kawaguchi Force conducted uncoordinated attacks on the night of the 12th after Japanese ships had shelled the ridge. Small bands of Japanese infiltrated through Marine strongpoints. Efforts were made to clear

9 See Battle Orders 12: *US Special Warfare Units in the Pacific Theater 1941–45.*

Marines of the 1st Parachute Battalion return enemy fire on Bougainville during the Koiari Beach raid. To the left is a Japanese 3.7cm Type 94 (1934) antitank gun turned on its former owners. Both Army and Marine paratroopers were trained to operate captured weapons.

1st Parachute Battalion Marines lie in hasty fighting positions during the Koiari Beach raid. A number of weapons are evident : a .45-cal. M55 SMG, a .45-cal. M1911A1 pistol, .30-cal. M1 carbines, and .30-cal. M1 rifles

the infiltrators in the morning, but resistance was heavy. The battalion pulled back further to the north of the ridge. After dark the Japanese launched repeated attacks. They created gaps and the understrength Marine companies were forced back into a tight perimeter. The position began to crumble and the parachute battalion acting Commanding Officer (CO) broke down to be replaced by the XO, Capt Harry L. Torgerson. He and other officers managed to rally the troops. The enemy disengaged at first light. The Marines attempted to regain lost positions, but were driven back and established a new line. Japanese attacks began again at nightfall, and continued through the night. At 0400 hours Edson requested the reserve 2/5 Marines be committed, and it moved up as artillery pounded the Japanese. Air strikes were called in at dawn and the Japanese effort was broken.

The Raiders suffered 135 casualties and the paratroopers 15 KIA and 113 WIA. Only 100 effectives remained. The Japanese lost 700 KIA and an estimated 500 WIA. Edson received the Medal of Honor for the defense of what became known as Edson's or Bloody Ridge. On September 17 the Raider-Parachute Battalion was dissolved and the 1st Parachute Battalion departed a couple of days later.

The unit moved to New Caledonia where it established Camp Kiser and rebuilt, practised jumps, and concentrated on jungle fighting and patroling. The 2d Parachute Battalion arrived on January 11, 1943. Plans were being made for the Central Solomons and the new 1st Battalion commander made an aerial reconnaissance of New Georgia. No suitable DZs were found though. The 1st Parachute Regiment was activated on New Caledonia in April.

Four combat jumps were considered, but all were canceled. The first was Kolombangara Island off the west end of New Georgia in July 1943. This would have supported the Army's landing on New Georgia to seize Munda Point, an operation expected to take ten days. Instead the operation became bogged down and required almost two months to complete. The paratroopers would have seized Villa Airfield, Kolombangara 16 miles to the northwest. It was realized they would have been stranded if the Munda attack bogged down. Another plan was to seize the Kahili and/or Kara airfields on southeast Bougainville in September. The original plan was for the 3d MarDiv and 35th InfDiv to land, but the area was far too heavily defended and instead the Marines landed at the more remote Torokina Cape on the lower southwest coast. Marine paratroopers would support this operation by conducting a diversion on Choiseul Island and the main landing itself (discussed below). A third operation was planned to seize Kavieng on the northwest end of New Ireland. This operation was part of the Allies' main effort in the area, to neutralize the Japanese naval and air base at

Rabaul, New Britain. The planned April 1944 operation was to be conducted by the 3d MarDiv and 40th InfDiv, but it was canceled in March. In August IMAC developed a plan to use paratroopers to seize the Japanese seaplane base at Rekata Bay, Santa Isabel, but the Japanese evacuated it in late September.

From June 1943, as the Allied offensive resumed, Marine and Army aircraft were no longer available for jumping. They were especially needed in New Guinea for airlifting troops over great distances, delivering supplies and equipment, for resupply drops, and medical evacuation. The 2d Battalion's last night jump in May saw the Army transports approach off course and drop the paratroopers into hilly jungle terrain, resulting in one dead and 11 injured. There were insufficient Marine R4D utility squadrons available (only seven in mid 1943), and three of them were still in the States training and one was in Hawaii. Even if all seven squadrons were concentrated together, they could only drop one and a half battalions. The 1st Parachute Regiment on New Caledonia focused on amphibious operations and would be useful for economy-of-force missions.

The next employment of the Marine paratroopers was the August 15, 1943 occupation of Vella Lavella north of New Georgia. The US Army and New Zealanders saw what little action there was. The 2d Battalion landed on the west-central coast with the IMAC Advance Echelon to establish a staging base on October 1. 2d Battalion's LST (landing ship, tank) was bombed on the beach and the unit lost 14 men and much of its supplies and equipment. They only provided security and patrolled the area. The rest of the 1st Parachute Regiment arrived in late October.

The 2d Parachute Battalion's turn for combat soon came. As a diversion for the November 1, 1943 Bougainville landing, the 2d Battalion would conduct a raid on Choiseul Island. This island, across The Slot from and north of Vella Levella, was used as a supply and barge staging base by the Japanese. The battalion was alerted on October 20 and would be landed on the upper northwest coast near Voza. The reinforced 725-man battalion would harass any enemy encountered and lead the enemy to believe that a larger force had landed. They would also reconnoiter for a PT boat base and withdraw after 12 days if it decided against the PT boat base. The unit's orders were "strike and move; avoid decisive engagement with superior forces."

Choiseul diversion, October–November 1943

2d Parachute Battalion (reinforced), 1st Parachute Regiment

  Machine Gun Platoon, Weapons Company, 1st Parachute Regiment

  Detachment, 1st Corps Experimental Rocket Platoon

  Detachment, Communication Platoon, HQ Company, 1st Parachute Regiment

---

An Australia-New Guinea Administrative Unit officer assembled 100 natives as guides and porters. Delivered by four destroyer-transports at 0030 hours, October 28, four LCP(R) (landing craft, personnel (ramp)) remained to shuttle the Marines along the coast and up rivers after the transports had departed. The nine men of the rocket detachment were armed with a tripod-mounted, eight-tube, 4.5in. T27E1 launcher and 40 rockets. Ashore by 0100 hours, a couple of single-plane air attacks materialized, but no damage was inflicted. While the landing craft (guarded by a platoon) were hidden at nearby Zinoa Island, the main force moved a mile into the hills to establish its base. Small patrols were sent out to locate enemy positions, and they attacked small elements. On the 30th companies E and F attacked a base at Sangigai and expended most of the rockets, killing over 70 Japanese. On November 1 Company G (less elements) moved by LCP(R) up the coast to the northwest. Known as the Bigger Patrol or

"Northwest Task Force," they attacked a barge base on Guppy Island, destroying a fuel dump. They then made several contacts with Japanese patrols and were withdrawn by landing craft in the evening. One boat was damaged on a reef, and drifted back to the shore that was swarming with Japanese. It was rescued by two PT boats under Lt John F. Kennedy. In the meantime, more patrols were dispatched by the main body and engaged enemy patrols. It was apparent the 3,000 enemy to the northwest and 1,800 to the southeast were now searching for the paratroopers. IMAC felt the battalion had accomplished its mission and could withdraw. The Bougainville landing was underway and it was obvious the Japanese were aware that it was the main landing. The diversion had been conducted too close to the Bougainville landing to allow the Japanese to divert troops to Choiseul, although some were being sent from Shortland Island. The Demolition Platoon had laid mines and booby traps to hamper enemy patrols and the Marines embarked aboard three LCIs (landing craft, infantry) at 0130 hours, November 5 and returned to Vella Lavella. The paratroopers had disrupted barge traffic, destroyed supplies, killed 150 Japanese, and captured a valuable minefield chart of The Slot. Their losses were 11 KIA and 14 WIA.

The 3d MarDiv landed at Cape Torokina on the lower southwest coast of Bougainville on November 1. After establishing a lodgment, the Japanese began counterattacking to drive the Americans off. The 1st Parachute Regiment on Vella Lavalla was the IMAC Reserve. The 1st Parachute Battalion arrived at Torokina on November 23 and was attached to the 2d Raider Regiment (Provisional), which was in reserve. To hinder the Japanese build up, a raid would be conducted on supply dumps at Koiari ten miles east of Cape Torokina on the west side of Empress Augusta Bay. It was to last not less than four days, and a decisive engagement was to be avoided. The 1st Parachute Battalion, reinforced by a Raider company, landed at 0400 hours, November 29 with 614 troops.

Koiari Beach raid, November 1943

1st Parachute Battalion (reinforced)

    Company M, 3d Raider Battalion

    Communication Detachment, IMAC Signal Battalion

    Two forward observer parties, 12th Marines

The headquarters and Raider companies landed 1,000 yards east of the main body. Resistance was heavy and it was not until 0930 hours that they linked up with the main body. The Raiders were to secure the beachhead while the paratroopers were to move inland. They were soon engaged by a much larger than expected enemy force, at least 1,200 infantry en route to the battle front. 155mm gunfire was directed from Cape Torokina. Ammunition was running low and there were communication problems. Resorting to Japanese weapons, and with darkness approaching together with an inevitable mass counterattack, the Navy made two attempts to extract the force, but was driven off by heavy fire. Covered by destroyers, the force was withdrawn at 2040 hours. Enemy dead were estimated at over 200. The Marines lost 17 KIA, seven missing in action (MIA), and 97 WIA plus many weapons. The battalion had lost 20 percent of its strength. Further raids had been planned, but were abandoned.

The 1st Parachute Regiment HQ Company, 3d Battalion, and Weapons Company arrived at Cape Torokina on December 4 aboard LCIs. On the 5th the regiment (less 1st and 2d battalions) was attached to the 3d MarDiv and directed to secure Hill 1000 on the northeast side of the perimeter. To accomplish this and cover its 3,000-yard sector with 900 men, the regiment formed the Provisional Parachute Battalion from a Headquarters Company detachment, the Weapons Company (less Company I), and Company I, 3d Battalion. 3d Battalion (less elements) occupied the south portion of the hill and the Provisional Battalion the north. Contact with enemy patrols began on the 8th and action continued through the day. Company C, 21st Marines reinforced the 3d Battalion that night. The Parachute Regiment was attached to the 9th Marines on the 9th, as it would occupy positions to the left of Hill 1000 on the 10th. Probes and patrols continued through the 10th until the Provisional Battalion was relieved by 1/9 Marines and 3d Battalion by 1/21 Marines. The Provisional Battalion was disbanded that day and the regiment became the 9th Marines reserve. The 3d Battalion remained the 9th Marines reserve while the 1st Battalion was attached to the 2d Raider Regiment. They were sent into the frontline on December 22, seeing some action. The 1st Parachute Regiment

Marine parachute unit commanders	
1st Marine Parachute Regiment	
Lt Col Robert H. Williams	1 April 43
Maj Richard Fagan	16 January–29 February 1944
1st Parachute Battalion	
Capt Marcellus J. Howard	15 August 1941
Maj Robert H. Williams	2 October 1941 (WIA)
Maj Charles A. Miller	8 August 1942 (relieved 12 September)
Capt Harry L. Torgerson	18 September 1942
Maj Brooke H. Hatch	1 April 1943
Maj Robert C. McDonough	28 April 1943
Maj Richard Fagan	10 May 1943
Maj Robert C. McDonough	11 January–29 February 1944
2d Parachute Battalion	
Maj Charles E. Shepard, Jr.	1 October 1941
Lt Col Richard W. Hayward	5 May 1942
Lt Col Victor H. Krulak	1 April 1943
Maj Warner T. Bigger	8 November 1943–29 February 1944
3d Parachute Battalion	
Maj Robert T. Vance	16 September 1942 (WIA)
Maj Harry L. Torgerson	10 December 1943–29 February 1944
4th Parachute Battalion	
Lt Col Marcellus J. Howard	1 July 1943
Maj Tom M. Trotti	1 October 1943–19 January 1944
Raider-Parachute Battalion	
Lt Col Merritt A. Edson (1st Raider Bn)	3–17 September 1942
Provisional Parachute Battalion	
Maj George R. Stallings	5–10 December 1943

Members of 1st Marine Parachute Regiment on Cape Torokina, Bougainville return from their fight at Hill 1000. This was to be the last action of the Marine paratroopers before they were disbanded and absorbed into the new 5th MarDiv being raised in the States.

departed Bougainville on January 12, 1944 for Guadalcanal where it joined the 2d Battalion from Vella Lavella, having arrived on the 2nd. Records are not clear on the number of casualties on Bougainville. Besides the casualties on the Koiari Beach raid they lost less than a dozen dead and over three dozen wounded.

These were the last actions of the Marine paratroopers. The 1st and 2d Battalions departed for San Diego on February 4 and the Regiment and 1st Battalion left on the 29th.

Nadzab, New Guinea

The 503d PIR departed Cairns, Australia for Port Moresby, Papua with the 2d Battalion being flown over on August 15, 1943. After eight months' training they were ready for action. The 1st and 3d battalions left aboard the Liberty ship SS *Duntroon* on the 20th and arrived on the 22nd. They bivouacked in Rigo Valley, where they continued tactical and jungle training. On September 1 the regiment was alerted for an operation.

The Markham Valley is located 250 miles north-northeast of Port Moresby in North-East New Guinea, spreading inland from the Huon Gulf. Nadzab village is on the north shore of the Markham River flowing through the 5 to 25-mile-wide valley. The Huron Peninsula lies to the northeast. The Japanese

Commanders, 503d Parachute Infantry Regiment, September 1943	
Regimental CO	Col Kenneth Kinsler
Regimental XO	Lt Col George M. Jones
1st Battalion	Maj Joe Lawrie
2d Battalion	Maj John Haltom
3d Battalion	Maj John J. Tolson III
Australian Army attachments	
Light Section, 2/4th Field Regiment	Lt J.N. Pearson
2/2nd Pioneer Battalion	Lt Col J.T. Lang
2/6th Field Co, Royal Australian Engineers	Lt S.L. Frew
B Co, Papuan Infantry Battalion	(no name available)
Note	
After the operation Jones commanded 1st Battalion and Lawrie was promoted to XO.	

still occupied Lea on the Huon Gulf and Finschhafen on the end of the peninsula. The Australians had driven the Japanese from most of the valley earlier, including Salamaua in the south. Resources were limited and a combination of overland movement, amphibious landing, and airlanding would be employed. The 9th Australian Division would land 18 miles east of Lea on the south coast of the Huron Peninsula on September 4 and advance on Lea. From upriver an Australian force would advance from Tsili Tsili, beginning on the August 30, to link up with the paratroopers. Lang's Force consisted of the 2/2nd Pioneer Battalion; 2/6th Field Company, Royal Australian Engineers;[10] B Company, Papuan Infantry Battalion; and 760 native bearers.

The 503d PIR would jump on to the abandoned Nadzab Airdrome 17 miles west of Lea on the morning of September 5 (Z-Day). The 7th Australian Division and the US 871st Airborne Engineer Battalion would be flown into the strip, once it had been made operational by Lang's Force. The 7th Division would advance on Lea to catch the Japanese in a pincer movement between itself and the 9th Division advancing from the east.

The 503d would be supported by 96 C-47s of the 317th TC Group. The group practiced the flight formation for three days before the jump. The 503d's strength was down owing to illness, training injuries, and a lack of replacements. The 1,700 paratroopers would be lifted by 79 C-47s while the rest carried supplies and equipment bundles plus an Australian 25-pdr howitzer section. This was to be the only full-regiment jump delivered in one lift in the PTO.

302 aircraft took off from airdromes around Port Moresby to participate in the operation. In the lead were six squadrons of B-25 bombers (armed with eight .50-cal. nose guns, 60 fragmentation bombs), which would strafe the drop zone (DZ) and surrounding area in waves. Three A-20 attack bombers on

Paratroopers of the 503d PIR en route to Nadzab, northeast New Guinea. This first US combat jump in the Pacific was one of the most effectively conducted. The paratroopers wear T-5 troop parachutes with B-4 life vests. Helmets would be donned and smokes extinguished ten minutes out from the DZ.

---

[10] Australian Imperial Force units (volunteer units were permitted to serve overseas; conscripts were not) prefixed by "2/" identify them as the second reiteration, as they had previously served in World War I.

Nadzab, September 5, 1943. The 503d PIR jumps from 500ft into Markham Valley to secure an airfield and block a Japanese withdrawal route. The smoke screen on the flank was laid down by A-20 attack bombers.

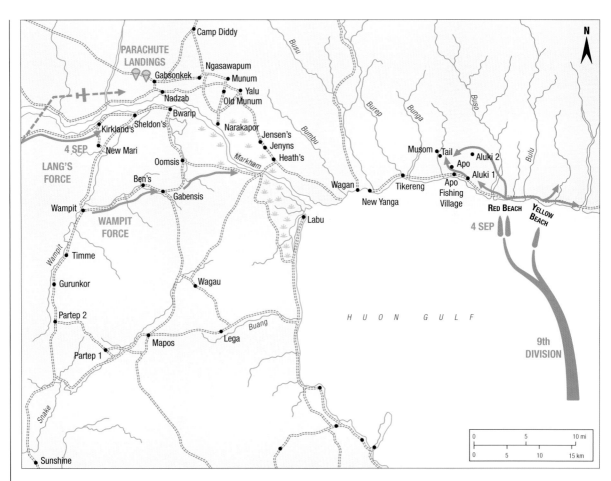

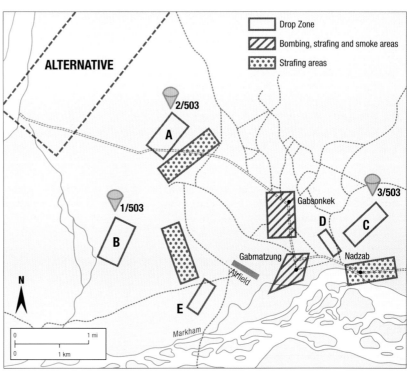

ABOVE Nadzab, New Guinea, 503d
Parachute Infantry Regiment,
September 5, 1943.

RIGHT The parachute landings
around Nadzab.

either side of the C-47 route would lay smoke screens on both sides of the DZs, while fighters flew cover. The transports took off at 0825 after a brief rain delay. After crossing the Owen Stanley Mountains the three transport flights descended to 500ft to arrive over Nadzab, with the first jumpers exiting at 1022 hours from 600ft. All troops were dropped in under five minutes with the 1st, 2d, and 3d battalions on Fields (DZs) B, A, and C, respectively. The Regimental Headquarters and Service Companies jumped on Field B and the artillery section on Field F.

There was no enemy in the area, but the troops suffered three jump fatalities and 33 injuries. Assembly was difficult in the 6–10ft-high kunai grass. 1/503d secured the abandoned airdrome, cleared obstacles, and guided in Lang's Force from Tsili Tsili. 2/503d secured Gabsonkek and blocked the north and northwest approaches. 3/503d secured Gabmatzung and established a blocking position on the trail to Japanese-held Lea. At 1230 hours 17 transports delivered supplies and the Australian artillery section. Five B-17 bombers later dropped 15 tons of supplies. In the late afternoon Lang's Force arrived and were attached to the 503d. Overnight they readied the airstrip to accept transports. The paratroopers' first use of flamethrowers was to burn kunai grass off the airstrip. Unfortunately the fire became out of control and destroyed hundreds of valuable unrecovered parachutes. The 871st Airborne Engineer Battalion was airlanded on the 6th and on the same day the lead elements of the 7th Division arrived. The division relieved the 503d on the 10th and two new extended airstrips were operational by the 14th. The operation was a complete success, leading MacArthur to declare it "the greatest example of combat efficiency he had ever witnessed."

Bad weather delayed the arrival of all 7th Division elements and the return of the 503d to base. On September 14, 3/503d was dispatched east behind the 25th Australian Brigade, to which it was attached, pushing toward Lea. The battalion secured the brigade's line of communication and north flank. The 1st Battalion was airlifted back to Port Moresby on the same day, soon followed by the 2d. The Japanese were withdrawing north from Lea and on the 15th 3/503d made contact. In the resulting firefights the paratroopers lost eight KIA and 12 WIA. Other casualties at Nadzab were 26 illness and non-battle injuries. While the Australians pursued the Japanese, 3/503d returned to Nadzab and was flown to Port Moresby on the 19th.

Eleven CG-5A gliders loaded with Australian engineers were on standby at Port Moresby in case Lang's Force did not reach Nadzab, but the lift was canceled.[11]

Unit strength was suffering and in October detachments from each 503d unit were sent back to Gordonvale to train 400 replacements. On October 20 the regimental commander committed suicide for no apparent reason and Lt Col George M. Jones took over. The unit implemented lessons learned, absorbed replacements, and continued training.

Planning began for the 503d's next operation, the capture of Cape Gloucester on the west end of New Britain, part of the effort to neutralize the Japanese base at Rabaul on the island's northeast end. The 1st MarDiv would land on December 26, 1943. The operation was under the Sixth Army and the 503d was attached. The regiment would be dropped onto two abandoned airstrips on the water's edge, a dangerous prospect. The 503d would have to be ferried to Dobadura, Papua forcing a bomber squadron to relocate owing to lack of space, and then dropped piecemeal on Cape Gloucester. It was a poor plan and disliked by Sixth Army and 1st MarDiv commanders. The Marines feared friendly fire casualties with the paratroopers dropping on the airfields and the Marines coming ashore so near. It was planned mainly because the Sixth Army commander thought he was expected to employ the regiment since it was

Australian parachute artillery
As the 503d PIR lacked artillery the commander of 2/4th Field Regiment, Royal Australian Artillery proposed detailing two of its new short 25-pdr (88mm) Mk I (Aust) gun-howitzers on the light (Aust) carriages. These were specially modified, Australian-made versions of the standard Commonwealth light artillery piece. Volunteers from the unit's three batteries were called to undertake an intense physical training course without being told it involved parachuting. Physical preparation began on August 17. On the 22nd the four officers and 30 enlisted reported to 1/503d. When it was found they had not been told the mission required parachuting, the 503d CO said any could withdraw; none did. They were hurriedly jump trained at Thirty-mile Strip outside Port Moresby and made one practice jump on the 30th, including dropping one gun, resulting in one officer and two enlisted injured. The officer replacement and a few enlisted who missed the practice jump made their first jumps on Z-Day over Nadzab. The 32-man Light Section, 2/4th Field Regiment was dropped from five C-47s at 1230 hours. The gunners were in the first two planes and the guns, ammunition, and equipment in the last three. A B-17 dropped another 192 rounds of ammunition at 1530 hours. One gunner was injured and one gun was operational in an hour. It took five days to locate all the second gun's components. Officer forward observers with American radios were dispatched to the parachute battalions. The artillery section never had the opportunity to fire a shot in anger. Upon arrival of the 25th Australian Brigade airlifted in the next day, the section was attached to 54 Battery, 2/4th Field Regiment.

---

11 The first glider pilots and mechanics to deploy to the PTO arrived in Australia in February 1943, followed by more in April. There was so little need for them that some were assigned other duties in troop carrier units and some returned to the States.

attached, but this was not the case. The mission was canceled. The regiment was relocated to Camp Cable 30 miles from Brisbane, Australian on February 2, 1944 and continued training.

On April 8 the regiment departed by ship and arrived at Dobadura near the east end of Papua's north coast. MacArthur's forces were working their way along the north coast of North-East New Guinea, bypassing and cutting off some Japanese lodgments and attacking the weaker ones. A two-division enveloping landing would occur on April 22 (D-Day), at Hollandia, Netherlands New Guinea, which was a major Japanese supply base. It was considered to drop in the 503d on to the three inland airstrips near Lake Sentami. This was canceled when it could not be determined if sufficient engineers could be flown in to make the airstrips operational in a shorter time than the amphibious forces could reach them, which they did four days after the landing. The 503d, in Sixth Army Reserve, was flown into Cyclops Airdrome on the 28th. It secured abandoned supply dumps, airstrips, and higher headquarters, as well as patrolled and mopped up over a wide area surrounding the new Allied base. In the process they killed 56 Japanese and took 12 prisoners, suffering one WIA.

The regiment was able to work its troops in a modest combat environment that helped integrate the replacements, and conducted further training. The unit's strength was now 2,146. It received its orders for the Noemfoor Island operation on June 28, 1944. Packed parachutes were delivered from the rear base at Gordonvale.

Noemfoor Island

Biak and Noemfoor islands are located in Geelvink Bay near the west end of Netherlands New Guinea. The Japanese were building airstrips on both islands. The Allies decided that their own airfields on these islands could support the coming Mariana Islands campaign. Army troops landed on Biak on May 27, 1944 and a hard fight ensued. The 503d PIR was tasked as a sea-delivered reserve, but was not needed. Fighting continued there through August, and it was determined the rebuilt airfields would not be ready to support the Marianas. Smaller Noemfoor to the west was selected for building the airfields, and to deny the Japanese a staging base to reinforce Biak from mainland New Guinea. The US operation was codenamed *Table Tennis*.

The 158th Infantry Regiment (Separate) conducted an amphibious landing on July 2, 1944 (D-Day) with the 503rd PIR in reserve at Cyclops Airdrome at Hollandia. Because of the lack of information on the strength of the island's defenders, how much resistance they might offer, and the need to secure the island rapidly to allow its three Japanese-built airstrips to be rebuilt quickly, the 503d would jump in; they were notified of this on June 28. Due to limits on the number of landing craft, it was not practical to ferry the 503d overwater, as the turnaround time was too great. Nor could aircraft land them, because of the presence of mud and craters on the airstrips; unloading and turnaround space on the airstrip was limited too, and would have caused severe ground congestion with incoming and outgoing flights. This was another reason parachute delivery of reinforcement was viable; it placed a large number of troops on the ground very quickly. Owing to aircraft shortages, only 38 were available from the 317th TC Group; one of the regiment's three battalions would be dropped each day between the 3rd and the 5th.

Troops of 1st Battalion, 503d PIR drop on to Kamiri Airdrome, Noemfoor Island. Jump injuries were high and even though vehicles were moved and other clear-up efforts undertaken, the 3/503d's jump the next day suffered almost as many casualties.

Commanders, 503d Parachute Infantry Regiment, July 1944	
Regimental CO	Col George M. Jones
Regimental XO	Lt Col Joe Lawrie
1st Battalion	Maj Cameron Knox
2d Battalion	Lt Col John W. Britten
3d Battalion	Maj John R. Erickson

The amphibious landing was at Kamiri Airdrome on the northwest side, and it was captured immediately, the enemy having withdrawn into the island's dense interior. More troops were quickly needed. 1/503d flew out of Hollandia, taking off at 0630 hours, and jumped 739 men, including elements of the Headquarters and Service Companies, at 1000 hours on D+1. The 400ft-altitude drop was not without hazards (the two lead aircraft were at 175ft having failed to reset their altimeters). The 250 x 5,000ft Kamiri Airdrome was immediately adjacent to the sea on the island's northwest coast; the area around it was covered with trees, Japanese aircraft wreckage, US amtracs, bulldozers, trucks, ammunition and supply dumps. Beneath the runway's mud covering was rock-hard coral. There were 72 jump injuries; nonetheless, the battalion deployed into the jungle.

Efforts were made to clear the wreckage and reposition equipment, but as 3/503d, plus elements of Headquarters and Service Companies, jumped the next day from a single column of C-47s rather than Vs, its 685 men suffered 56 injuries. All told, 59 men out of 1,424 suffered multiple fractures and numerous leaders through the chain-of-command were injured. 2/503d's July 5 jump was canceled and it was delivered by LCI at 1115 hours on July 11 at Roemboi Bay on the southwest coast after being airlifted from Hollandia to Biak 60 miles away. While the two battalions suffered 9 percent casualties, their timely introduction sped up the securing of the island. On July 6 a 2/503d detachment provided security as a radar site was established on Manin Island, three miles west of Noemfoor.

The 503d PIR was assigned the southern half of the island to clear, while the 158th Infantry cleared the north. Battery A, 147th Field Artillery Battalion (105mm) was attached to the 503d from July 14 until the operation's completion. The Japanese were scattered in small groups and made every effort to evade contact. The extensive patroling resulted in numerous firefights. The island was

Troops of 2d Battalion, 503d PIR wait for LCIs to haul them to Noemfoor. Their jump on to Noemfoor was canceled following the 1st and 3d battalions high jump-injury rate during the reinforcement jumps.

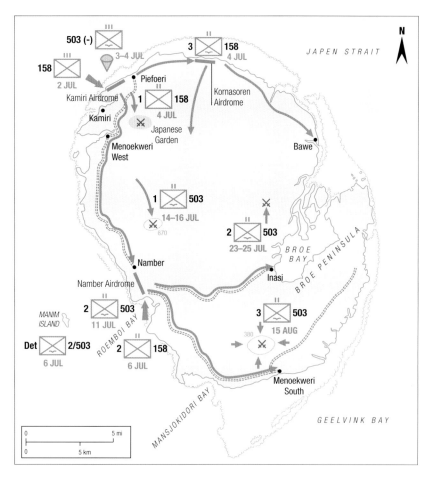

Noemfoor Island, 503d Parachute Infantry Regiment, July–August, 1944.

declared secure on August 31. The 158th continued to mop up into January 1945. Besides the initial jump casualties, the 503d lost 39 KIA, 72 WIA, and over 400 sick and injured, but killed over 1,000 Japanese and took 82 prisoners.

The 602-man 462d PFAB (which arrived on August 7), and the 138-man Company C (Parachute), 161st Airborne Engineer Battalion (which had arrived a few days earlier) were assigned to what was now the 503d PRCT in late August. The unit remained on Noemfoor, inhabiting a camp built by its engineers where it conducted training and practice jumps.

Initial plans for the reconquest of the Philippines called for a landing on Mindanao in October and another on Leyte in November. On September 2 the 503d was assigned an airborne mission on Leyte, to be executed on November 15. This was canceled on September 15 and a week later the plan altered for a landing directly on Leyte, with the 503d arriving at a later date by sea as a reaction force.

The 503d departed Noemfoor on November 13 aboard two troop ships, landing on Leyte on the 19th. They established a base camp near the Burauen Airfields and set up beach defenses to prevent a counterlanding. Their only action resulted from the crashlanding of three Japanese transports bearing paratroopers bound for targets to the north on November 26. Those not killed outright were hunted down. The US effort to refurbish and build new airstrips for the approaching Luzon campaign was hampered by the weather and Japanese air attacks.

It was decided that Mindoro to the south, near Luzon, had to be taken and airfields built to support Luzon. The 503d was alerted for a parachute assault on December 5 (U-Day), but the lack of transports, and fighter cover, and the proximity of significant Japanese air forces on Luzon brought about the cancelation of the operation. The 503d would execute an amphibious assault, Operation *Mike I*. The regiment embarked on December 11 and conducted a practice landing, which was their only amphibious training. Owing to deception efforts, the Japanese were not expecting the landing when the task force arrived off the southwest coast of Mindoro on the 15th. The objective was four airstrips near the coast; there was no intent to secure the entire island. The 503d landed on either side of the Bugasanga River on beaches Green and Blue at 0730 hours. The 19th Infantry (less elements), 24th InfDiv landed to the right. The lodgment was secured and there was little action. Through January 1945 several amphibious reconnaissance-in-force missions and raids were conducted about the island to harass the Japanese. The regiment's casualties on Mindoro were 16 KIA and 71 WIA.

On January 1 the regiment was transferred from Sixth to Eighth Army control. The 511th PIR arrived on Mindoro, established a camp near San José Airfield, and staged from there on February 3 for its first jump on Luzon. On January 25 the 503d was alerted for a mission to seize Nichols Field south of Manila, but this was canceled on February 5. The 11th AbnDiv was advancing toward the area and Japanese defenses were deemed too strong to parachute in a unit, which would be left exposed. It would require eight days before the 11th secured Nichols, which they finally did on the 12th. On the 6th the 503d was alerted for the Corregidor assault and transferred to Sixth Army.

Commanders, 503d Parachute Regimental Combat Team, August 1944	
Regimental CO	Col George M. Jones
Regimental XO	Lt Col Joe Lawrie
1st Battalion	Maj Cameron Knox
2d Battalion	Lt Col John W. Britten
3d Battalion	Maj John R. Erickson
462d PFAB	Lt Col Donald Madigan (injured September)
	Maj Arlis E. Kline
Company C, 161st Airborne Engineer Bn	Capt James S. Beyer

The Leyte operation

The 11th AbnDiv landed "administratively" on Leyte on November 18, 1944, almost a month after the initial October 20 landing (Operation *King II*), and a base camp was established at Bito. Now attached to XXIV Corps, the division relieved the 7th InfDiv at Burauen on the 21st and the 511th PIR was placed in the line with the 188th GIR securing the south flank. The 187th PIR with 674th and 675th GFABs, converted to infantry, secured airfields, retaining this status to the operation's end.

The divisional band was trained to operate Duck amphibious trucks. On November 29 three Japanese bombers carrying commandos crashlanded on San Pablo Airstrip, and the survivors were hunted down, although some escaped. The fighting in the jungle-covered hills in ceaseless rain was difficult, as the 511th pushed west across the island. Much of the resupply was accomplished by consolidating all the artillery battalions' L-4 and L-5 liaison aircraft at San Pablo. The 35 planes conducted countless resupply airdrops to units scattered in the mountains, delivering an average of 21 tons a day. A forward command, artillery, and supply base was established at Manarawat Ridge in the mountains. Carabao (water buffalo) were used to pack in supplies, but were too slow. Units were so scattered and the terrain so chaotic that it was difficult to determine where they were. There were several instances when

A 75mm M1A1 pack howitzer of Battery A, 457th PFAB in position on Manarawat Ridge, Leyte. The canvas trap offered protection from the intermittent sun and persistent rain. The four-gun battery was parachuted into the advanced base using a single C-47, which made 13 sorties.

individuals parachuted from L-5s as guides, replacements, or to take command of a stranded unit. During the operation 2/187th GIR was attached to the 511th and later 1/187th too.

The division's first combat jump was a piecemeal operation conducted between November 27 and December 4 (Operation *Tabletop*). As the 511th moved west it became more difficult to adjust artillery fire. Even 155mm guns of XXIV Corps Artillery provided support, but light artillery was necessary for close support. A howitzer battery was to be parachuted into the Manarawat base on December 4. It was realized the guns would be abandoned once the base was no longer of use. Twelve C-47s were required to drop a battery, but none were available, being dedicated to resupply and evacuation. A single C-47 was based at San Pablo for air–sea rescue. The pilot was persuaded to make 13 runs, dropping a howitzer or ammunition and equipment with gunners each sortie to deliver Battery A, 457th PFAB. After dropping the first load on a DZ two miles from Manarawat, the pilot felt he could successfully drop onto Manarawat itself, and did so. 1st Platoon, Company B, 1/187th GIR with 24 men dropped in advance of the battery using six L-4 and L-5 liaison airplanes. They made four lifts dropping one man at a time. On the same day a small division forward CP was parachuted from L-5s into Manarawat followed by the rest Company B, 187th GIR for base security and a platoon of Company C, 127th Airborne Engineer Battalion, which cleared an L-4 strip (but one too small for L-5s to land). Beginning November 27, small 511th Signal and 221st Medical Company elements, the Reconnaissance Platoon, and CP personnel were dropped – some 241 personnel in all.

At 1800 hours on December 5, the Japanese launched an ambitious operation in which ground elements infiltrated 11th AbnDiv positions and attacked the rear and airstrips, while 38 transports and bombers attempted to deliver 500 paratroopers of the 3d and 4th Raiding Regiments. Most of the aircraft were shot down and only 60 jumpers descended on San Pablo strip, where most were killed after inflicting minimal damage. Various divisional units mopped up, along with the briefly attached 38th InfDiv's 149th Infantry. The shock effect the Japanese counted on with raiders parachuting from the sky was lost on the 11th AbnDiv, to whom it appeared perfectly natural. It was the only instance in which paratroopers dropped on to another parachute unit.[12]

12 See Elite 127: *Japanese Paratroop Forces of World War II*.

The 511th with 2/187th GIR was now fighting its way down the west side of the mountains toward Ormac Bay. The 187th Headquarters was brought up to Manarawat in mid December to help control operations with 1/187th and 2/188th GIRs. The fighting was vicious, and made tougher by the terrain and weather. Pockets of resistance had to be destroyed in the "rear area." On December 22 the 511th made contact with the 7th InfDiv to the north. The 511th reached Ormac Bay on December 25. The last major fight was to overrun Purple Heart Hill north of Manarawat on the 27th. There was still much mopping up and patroling to be done, but between December 27 and January 15 the division was concentrated at Bito and readied to depart for Luzon. MacArthur complimented the division: "Operating in the central mountain regions southeast of Ormoc, the 11th Airborne has been wagging aggressive warfare along a wide sector. The Division has annihilated all resistance within the area."

The 11th killed 5,800 Japanese and took 12 prisoners while losing 168 KIA, 352 WIA, and 12 MIA. Levels of non-combat injuries and illness had been high. On the beach at Bito it rested, rebuilt, and trained, but no replacements arrived. It was reassigned to Eighth Army. The Sixth Army landed at Lingayen Gulf on west-central Luzon on January 9 and the 11th was alerted to prepare for operations to the south of Manila on the 22nd.

11th Airborne Division attachments on Leyte
1st Battalion (less elements), 306th Infantry Regiment, 77th InfDiv
1st Battalion, 382d Infantry Regiment, 96th InfDiv
Company B, 767th Tank Battalion [M4]
Battery D, 102d Antiaircraft Artillery Automatic Weapons Battalion (Air Transportable)
Cannon Company, 21st Infantry Regiment, 24th InfDiv[1]
5th & 7th Medical Portable Surgical Hospitals

Note
1 Armed with eight 105mm M7 self-propelled howitzers, the 21st Infantry had no need for the company, being employed to secure numerous small islands and sites scattered over a wide area.

In Leyte's rugged, rain-drenched hills vehicles could not traverse the native tracks leading to forward positions. Local civilians were hired by the 11th AbnDiv to carry supplies and ammunition forward. Here two boys bear a 10-in-1 ration (enough food for 10 men for one day) giving an idea of the manpower effort needed to sustain frontline units. A similar situation later confronted the 503d PIR on Negros Island.

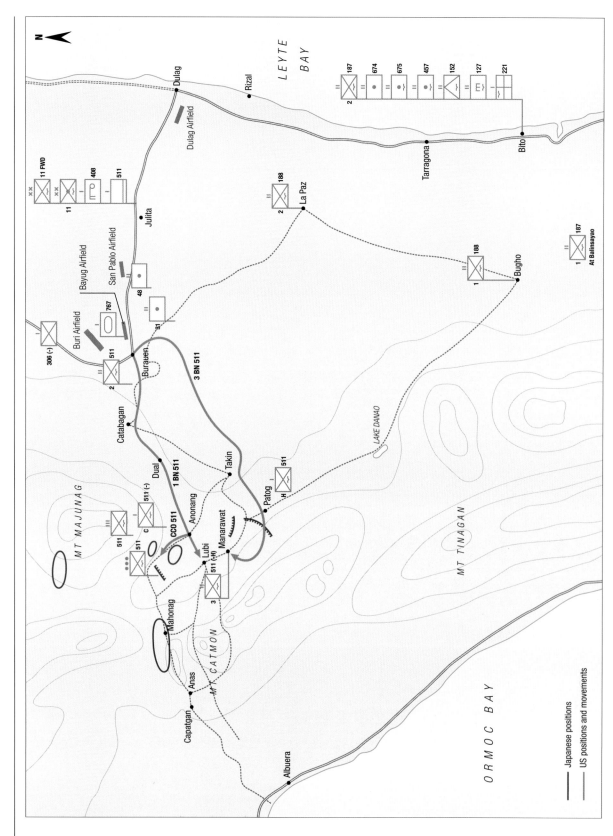

11th Airborne Division relieves 7th Infantry Division, Leyte, November 28, 1944.

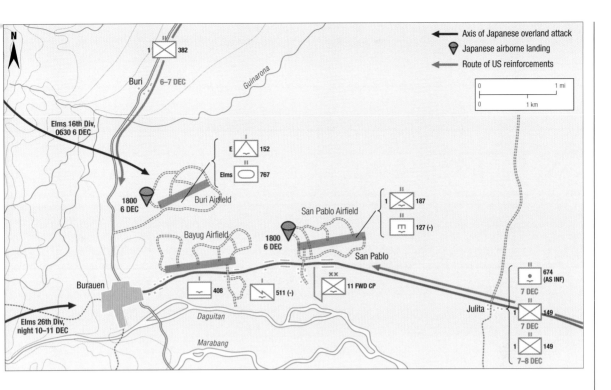

Japanese attacks on Burauen Airfields, December 6–11, 1944.

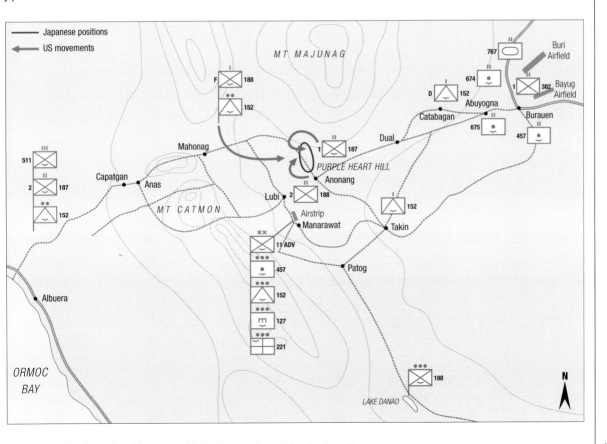

Purple Heart Hill, December 26–27, 1944. 11th Airborne Division's last battle on Leyte.

The Luzon operations

The first operation planned for the 11th AbnDiv on Luzon was developed by MacArthur's GHQ, and envisioned the 11th AbnDiv being dropped over southern Luzon in 200-man reinforced companies to confuse the enemy. This included the glider regiments, which would be provided with rudimentary parachute training for those not yet qualified. It was a foolish plan that prevented the division from massing its forces for decisive action and begged for the small scattered units to be cut off from resupply and annihilated. There were not enough aircraft to undertake the drop and any resupply efforts, much less to provide them close air support. Swing successfully resisted the plan. Another plan was for a parachute and glider assault on the Clark Field complex (11 airfields) north of Manila, but the gliders were still in shipping crates on a distant island (it required 250 man-hours to assemble a glider). Again, resupply would have been difficult in the mountain-surrounded valley, and as it was it took longer than anticipated for ground forces to reach the area. If the 511th alone parachuted onto Clark, it would be of insufficient strength. It was considered for the 503d PIR to be attached to the 11th for this mission, a plan approved by both Swing and the 503d commander, but GHQ held back the 503d for Corregidor. A plan evolved for the glider regiments to make an amphibious assault with a follow-on parachute assault. The division, minus the 511th PIR, departed Bito, Leyte on January 27, leaving a rear base.

The landing at Nasugbu just south of Manila Bay and 55 miles southwest of Manila was planned for January 31, 1945 (X-Day). The operation was codenamed *Mike VI*, and was to commence as a reconnaissance-in-force, with only a single regiment landed; if resistance was light, the rest of the division would land. The 188th GIR conducted a rehearsal at Bito before departing. The 187th GIR would be in reserve landing on order and undertook no rehearsal. The 511th PIR was moved to Mindoro by LCI and C-46 to stage at San José Airfield for its part of the operation. It would parachute onto Tagaytay Ridge 20 miles east of Nasugbu to secure Highway 17 running east then north to Manila, on which Sixth Army was advancing from the north (Operation *Shoestring*). The 511th would be delivered in three waves on January 2–3 so long as it was felt the division could reach the ridge within 24 hours after the drop. A battalion of the 19th Infantry, 24th InfDiv on Mindoro was the standby reserve.

The convoy departed Leyte on the 27th to arrive off Nasugbu at dawn on the 31st. 1/188th GIR went ashore on Beach Red at 0815 hours, experiencing

Carabao – Filipino water buffalo – were also used to haul supplies, but they were too slow, could not carry enough for their size, required more time to feed, water and graze than men, and could not negotiate extremely rugged terrain.

sporadic fire. It pushed inland and 2/188th landed to clear enemy positions on either flank. After noon it was decided resistance was light and 1/187th was sent ashore and attached to the 188th. 2/187th relieved 188th elements securing the flanks and they rejoined the regiment. Other units protecting the beachhead were the 152d AAA Battalion and Battery D, 102d AAA Battalion. The 188th, reinforced with 1/187th, 674th (less elements) and 675th GFABs,

11th Airborne Division commanders	
Division Commander	Maj Gen Joseph M. Swing
Assistant Division Commander	Brig Gen Albert Pierson
Chief of Staff	Col Francis W. Farrell
	Col Irvin R. Schimmelpfenning (KIA 4 February 1945)
	Col Michael Williams
511th Parachute Infantry Regiment	Col Orin D. Haugen (KIA 11 February 1945)
	Col Edward H. Lathi (WIA 8 February 1945)
1st Battalion	Lt Col Earnest LaFlamme (relieved January 1945)
	Maj Henry A. Burgess
2d Battalion	Lt Col Norman M. Shipley (WIA)
	Lt Col Frank S. Holcombe
3d Battalion	Lt Col Edward H. Lathi
	Lt Col John Strong
187th Glider Infantry Regiment	Col Harry Hildebrand (to 15 March 1945)
	Col George Pearson
1st Battalion	Lt Col George Pearson (to 187th XO January 1945)
	Lt Col Harry Wilson
2d Battalion	Lt Col Norman E. Tipton
	Lt Col Harry Wilson (to 1/187th January 1945)
	Lt Col Norman E. Tipton
188th Glider Infantry Regiment	Col Robert H. Soule (WIA 2 February 1945, promoted out of division 1 March 1945)
	Col Norman E. Tipton
1st Battalion	Lt Col Earnest LaFlamme
2d Battalion	Lt Col Thomas L. Mann
Division Artillery	Brig Gen Wyburn D. Brown
	Brig Gen Francis W. Farrell (ill 15 August 1945)
	Brig Gen Frank Dorn
457th Parachute Field Artillery Battalion	Lt Col Douglass P. Quandt
	Lt Col Nicholas G. Stadtherr
674th Glider Field Artillery Battalion	Lt Col Lucas E. Hoska, Jr.
675th Glider Field Artillery Battalion	Lt Col Ernest L. Massad
152d Airborne Antiaircraft Battalion	Lt Col James H. Farren
127th Airborne Engineer Battalion	Lt Col Douglas C. Davis
Provisional Reconnaissance Platoon	1st Lt Polka
	1st Lt George Skau (died August 1945)

Note
Change of command dates are not always available.

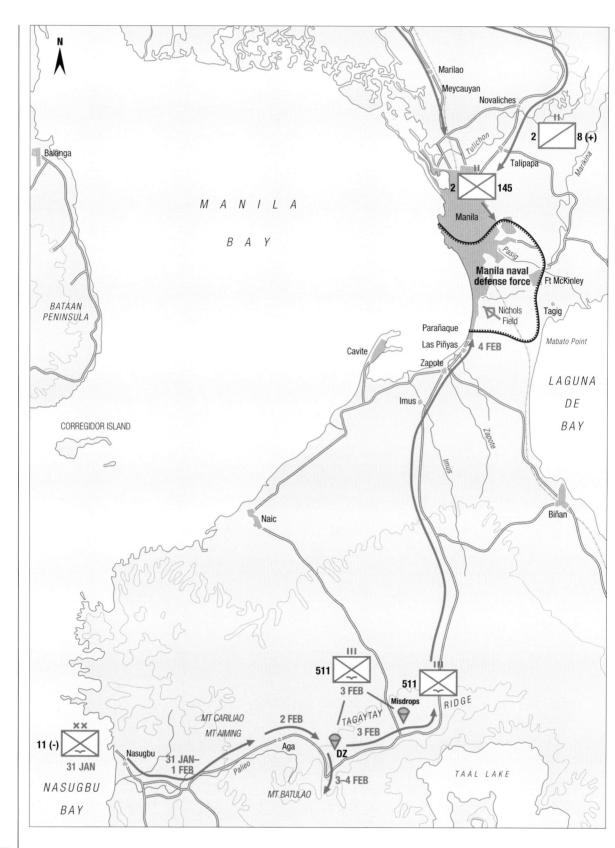

N

Balanga

MANILA

BAY

BATAAN
PENINSULA

CORREGIDOR ISLAND

Marilao

Meycauyan

Novaliches

Tulichon

Marikina

2   8 (+)

Talipapa

2   145

Manila

Pasig

Manila naval
defense force

Ft McKinley

Nichols
Field

Tagig

Parañaque

Las Piñyas

Mabato Point

4 FEB

LAGUNA

DE

BAY

Cavite

Zapote

Imus

Imus

Zapote

Naic

Biñan

511

3 FEB

511

Misdrops

RIDGE

MT CARILIAO

MT AIMING

2 FEB

TAGAYTAY

3 FEB

11 (-)

Nasugbu

31 JAN–
1 FEB

Palico

Aga

DZ

MT BATULAO

3–4 FEB

TAAL LAKE

31 JAN

NASUGBU

BAY

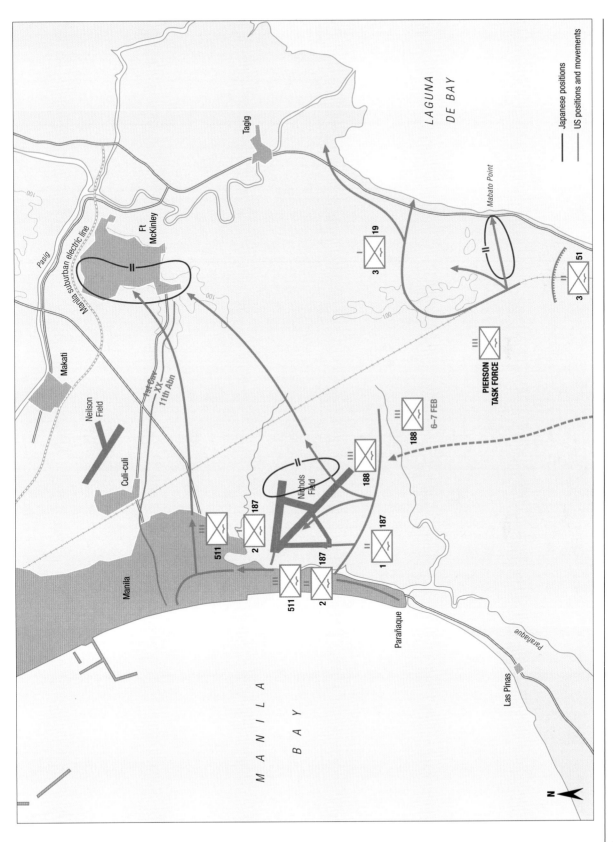

LAGUNA DE BAY

Tagig

Ft McKinley

Pasig

Manila suburban electric line

Makati

Neilson Field

Culi-culi

Manila

MANILA BAY

Nichols Field

1st Bn
XX
11th Abn

Mabato Point

3 | 19

3 | 51

PIERSON TASK FORCE

188
6–7 FEB

188

187

187
1

187
2

511
2

187

511

Parañaque

Las Pinas

Parañaque

N

Japanese positions
US positions and movements

11th Airborne Division, cracking the Genko Line, February 4–21, 1945.

127th Engineer Battalion elements, and Battery D, 457th PFAB, pressed inland on Highway 17. The west end of Tagaytay Ridge was reached after midnight and the advance slowed owing to increasing resistance. The jump was rescheduled for the 3rd–4th because of the delay. The Reconnaissance Platoon followed a trail north of the highway to determine enemy strength. 511th's Demolition Platoon, serving as pathfinders, infiltrated over another trail to reach Tagaytay Ridge and mark the DZ. At 0730 hours, February 3, the 188th would attack eastward up Highway 71, which followed the crest of the eight-mile-long, 1,880ft-high Tagaytay Ridge. The 511th would parachute on to the ridge near its west end and attack westward to trap the Japanese rear holding up the 188th. This was one of the few good DZs used in the Pacific, 2,000 x 4,000 yards and being mostly cultivated fields. Guerrillas had mostly cleared out the Japanese.

With only forty-eight 317th TC Group C-47s available, a third of what was needed to lift the regiment, the 511th PIR, a platoon of the 221st Medical Company, and a squad of the 127th Engineer Battalion boarded its transports on Mindoro. Prior to the first lift 240 parachutes with dummies were dropped near Mount Malepunyo 20 miles southwest of Tagaytay Ridge to draw any Japanese fighters. The first lift came over Lake Teal from the south. At 0815 hours the 346 troopers jumped from 18 C-47s onto the ridge, which was marked by the pathfinders' green smoke grenades. The next lift of 570 men in 30 aircraft was dropped 8,000 yards east-northeast of the DZ and further along the ridge because of the premature release of bundles from one aircraft. The third lift of 51 aircraft, using the first two lifts' transports, dropped at 1210 hours. Eighty men landed on the DZ, but the following aircraft saw the grounded parachutes of the first misdropped lift, and jumped in the same place. There were no enemy in the area and the regiment was able to assemble on the DZ in five hours. The 511th linked up with the 188th at 1300 hours. The 457th PFAB and support elements were dropped the next morning at 0815 hours. A total of 1,830 men (or 1,750, according to conflicting sources) jumped, with injuries amounting to some 50 lightly injured and one killed.

By mid afternoon seventeen 2½-ton trucks arrived from the beach, and 2/511th boarded to follow the now jeep-mounted Reconnaissance Platoon, which was reporting the road clear of resistance. The trucks would shuttle troops forward as the rest marched north toward Manila. By midnight of the 4th the lead elements were on the southern outskirts of the city and 70 miles from the beachhead. Casualties up to this point were 35 KIA and 150 WIA.

Halted at Parañaque, the division now faced the well-developed Genko Line, an in-depth position with 1,200 pillboxes backed by artillery on the south side of Manila stretching from Nichols Field on Manila Bay inland to Ft. William McKinley and tied into Laguna de Bay. With the 511th on the left with 2/187th attached, and 188th on the right with 1/187th attached, the division attacked into the Japanese positions. The division CP was in Parañaque on the coast just south of enemy lines. The fighting was vicious, and the lines took almost three weeks to break through. It took from February

---

Task Force Pierson, February 1945

1st Battalion, 187th GIR

3d Battalion, 19th Infantry Regiment, 24th InfDiv

457th PFAB (less Battery C)

Company A, 44th Tank Battalion [M4]

Platoon, Company A, 127th Airborne Engineer Battalion

Platoon, 221st Airborne Medical Company

7 to 12 to take Nichols. Contact was made with 1st CavDiv patrols from the north on the 11th and that day the 11th AbnDiv was reassigned to Sixth Army and XIV Corps. To clear the shore of Laguna de Bay, Task Force Pierson was formed on February 14 under the assistant division commander; it became Pearson Task Force, being named after the 1/187th GIR commander, \on the 20th. It took from the 18th to the 23rd to clear the area.

Having taken Nichols, the rest of the division attacked northeast to seize Ft. McKinley, which took from the 13th–19th to secure. Cavite Naval Ammunition Depot on Manila Bay was secured by division Special Troops on the 21st. The Los Baños raid was executed on the 23rd (described below). On the 24th the division was re-tasked to clear southern Luzon. Through this operation the division's rear area was secured by 187th GIR with the 1/19th Infantry; 152d Airborne AA Battalion; Battery C, 457th PFAB; and guerrillas. Total division causalities were 210 KIA and 750 WIA.

Corregidor

XI Corps had broken organized resistance on Bataan on the west side of Manila Bay on February 16, 1945. Mopping up continued, but now the stage was set for opening the bay and the port of Manila. The 11th AbnDiv would secure the east side of the bay on the 21st and the battle for Manila would conclude on March 3. To open the bay the four fortified islands in its mouth had to be seized. Predominant among these was Corregidor. While the original US guns on "the Rock," as it was known, were inoperable, the defenders would be able to harass shipping entering the bay. Corregidor was a symbol of American resistance in the war's early dark days, and MacArthur wished it to be recaptured with flair. Planning began by Sixth Army on February 3 and a combined parachute and amphibious assault would be executed on the 16th. An amphibious-only assault was thought too costly and would require a large number of troops. On Mindoro the 503d PRCT was alerted on February 6 to provide the core of the Rock Force under XI Corps.

Corregidor is two miles off the east end of Bataan, and is tadpole shaped, being 3½ miles long and 1½ miles across at its west end. Its surface is uneven and rugged and its long tail offered a DZ at Kindley Field, a small overgrown airstrip; however, this was too narrow and too close to the water, and the paratroopers would have to attack uphill from Bottomside near water level to Middleside, a small plateau part way up the side to even higher Topside on the western lobe. Topside offered two small DZs, but was edged by 400–500ft cliffs with numerous buildings and gun positions scattered across it with trees, craters, and rubble.

Artillerymen of the 462d PFAB on Corregidor search for Japanese snipers as they ready their 75mm M1A1 pack howitzers. All 12 of the battalion's guns were dropped on to the island without damage. They were used for direct fire against enemy positions and later in the indirect-fire role on the island's tail.

503d Parachute Regimental Combat Team on Corregidor, February 16, 1945.

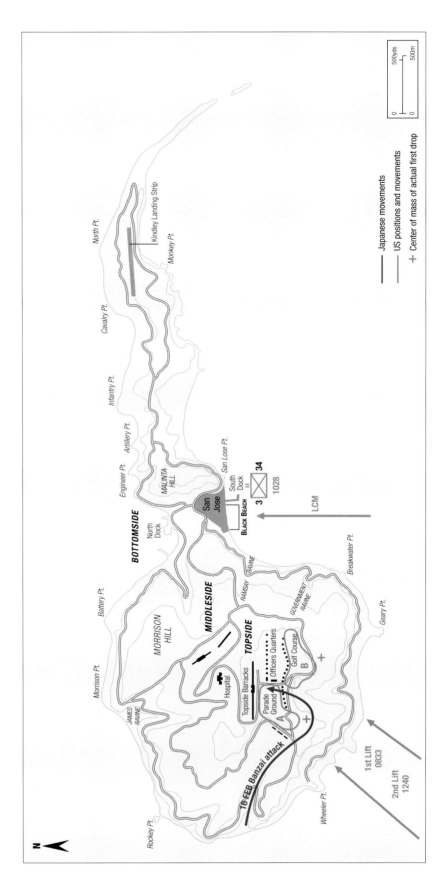

Rock Force, 503d PRCT, Corregidor, February 1945

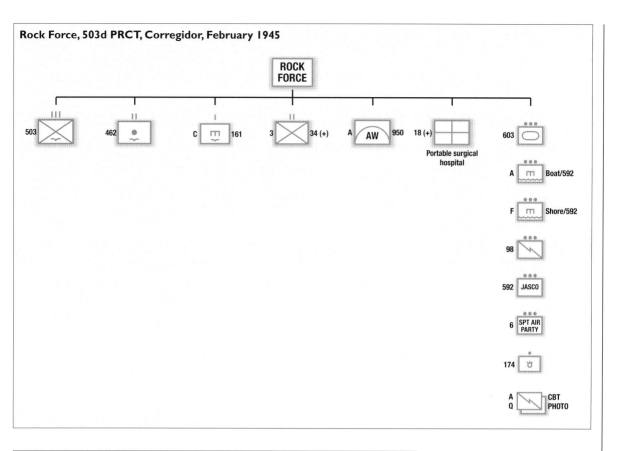

Rock Force – 503d Parachute Regimental Combat Team (reinforced)
503d Parachute Infantry Regiment
462d Parachute Field Artillery Battalion
Company C (Parachute), 161st Airborne Engineer Battalion
3d Battalion, 34th Infantry Regiment, 24th InfDiv
Company A, 1st Battalion, 34th Infantry Regiment
3d Platoon, Antitank Company, 34th Infantry Regiment
3d Platoon, Cannon Company, 34th Infantry Regiment [3 x M7]
3d Platoon, Company C, 3d Engineer Combat Battalion
3d Platoon, Company C, 24th Medical Battalion
Detachment, Service Company, 34th Infantry Regiment
Battery A, 950th Antiaircraft Artillery Automatic Weapons Battalion
Detachment, 1st Platoon, 603d Medium Tank Company, 1st CavDiv [2 x M4]
Detachment, Company A, Boat Battalion, 592d Engineer Boat & Shore Regiment
Detachment, Company F, Shore Battalion, 592d Engineer Boat & Shore Regiment
Detachment, 98th Signal Battalion
Detachment, 592d Joint Assault Signal Company
Detachment, 6th Support Air Party
Squad, 174th Ordnance Detachment (Bomb Disposal)
Combat Photography Units A & Q, GHQ Signal Section
18th Medical Portable Surgical Hospital (reinforced)

Commanders, 503d Parachute Regimental Combat Team, February 1945	
Regimental CO	Col George M. Jones (injured 16 February)
Regimental Deputy CO[1]	Lt Col John J. Tolson III (WIA 16 February)[1]
Regimental XO	Lt Col Joe Lawrie
1st Battalion	Maj Robert H. Woods (KIA 24 February)
	Maj John N. Davis
2d Battalion	Maj Lawson B. Caskey
3d Battalion	Lt Col John R. Erickson
462d PFAB	Maj Arlis E. Kline (injured 16 February)
	Maj Melvin R. Knudson
Company C, 161st Airborne Engineer Bn	Capt James S. Beyer
3d Battalion, 34th Infantry Regiment	Lt Col Edward M. Postlethwait[2]

Notes

1 The former 3/503d CO was assigned to Sixth Army G-3 Section and borrowed as deputy CO and observer for the Rock assault. He was instrumental in encouraging and planning the assault. Tolson was injured in the second lift jump and evacuated four days later.

2 Postelthwait attended the Airborne Course after the war and commanded the 503d AIR in Germany in 1957.

The plan was to heavily bomb and shell the island and then parachute a battalion onto Topside at 0830 hours, February 16, which it was suspected the Japanese had not considered. Once Topside was secured the attackers would dominate the rest of the island including the 390ft-high Malinta Hill and its tunnel complex at the base of the tail. The challenges of the jump were like none other before or since. Winds were expected to be from the east at 15–25mph. The transports would only be over their DZ for six seconds dropping six to eight jumpers. Each plane would have to make three passes. A jumper dropped 400ft above Topside (950ft above sea level) could drift about 250ft. There was little room for error and it was expected jumpers would drift into the sea or get caught up on the cliff sides. The transports would make their run in two columns, one over each DZ, approaching from the southeast. It would require an hour to drop the first lift. The aircraft would return to Mindoro for the second lift, which would not be on the ground until five hours after the first jumpers exited. As always, insufficient aircraft were available. Casualties were expected to be 20–50 percent, jump and combat, if surprise were achieved. The 503d had insufficient serviceable parachutes on hand, and the 11th AbnDiv provided 1,500 of them.

First lift
HQ & HQ Company (less elements), 503d Parachute Infantry Regiment
3d Battalion, 503d Parachute Infantry Regiment
HQ & HQ Battery (less elements), 462d Parachute Field Artillery Battalion
Battery C, 462d Parachute Field Artillery Battalion
3d Platoon, Battery D, 162d Parachute Field Artillery Battalion
3d Platoon, Company C, 161st Airborne Engineer Battalion

It was expected that a direct amphibious assault would result in higher casualties. The Japanese were in fact deployed for a sea attack and had not erected antiairborne obstacles. Rather than the expected 850 defenders though, there were 5,000–6,000 SNLF, naval base and service personnel organized into combat units and a few army troops. At 1030 hours an infantry battalion would land at Bottomside from the south. It would seize a beachhead, make contact with the paratroopers on Topside, and block enemy movement from the tail and the Malinta Hill tunnel; more importantly, it would open up an over-water resupply and casualty evacuation route. This would also provide a base from which to attack Malinta Hill. The second parachute lift would drop on the same DZs at 1215 hours and take over DZ security from the first lift. The third battalion was prepared for parachute or landing craft delivery on the 17th.

DZ A was the 250 x 325-yard parade ground in front of the "Mile-Long Barracks." DZ B was just to the southeast, on the nine-hole, 185 x 350-yard golf course.

Aerial bombardment of Corregidor had commenced on January 22 and by the day of the attack 3,125 tons of explosives had rained down on the island from the air and the sea. Before the transports arrived, 24 B-24s, 11 B-25s, and 31 A-20s struck the island. Just prior to the jump 70 A-20s mass-strafed the Rock.

At dawn the first lift departed San Josè and Elmore airfields, Mindoro aboard 54 317th TC Group C-47s. Among them were ten non-parachute qualified volunteers: joint assault signal company, support aircraft party, photographers, and an interpreter.[13] The second and third lifts' rifle company XOs jumped with the first to coordinate and brief their companies upon arrival. The regimental XO remained with the third lift supervising follow-on lift loading.

Approaching from the southwest the jump commenced at 0833 hours and by 0945 hours units were assembled. Fire was light and the small number of enemy were killed or driven off. Some 25 percent of the first lift were injured or failed to land on the DZ. Early passes were dropped from 550–600ft rather than 400ft and the winds were over 20mph. Later passes were lower, improving accuracy. The center of mass of the first drops fell just to the south of both DZs. Men were caught up on the cliffs south and southwest of the DZs. Some landed on the narrow beach at the foot of the cliffs and others went into the bay, but

Troops of the 1/503d PIR "chute up" for the Corregidor jump at San Josè Airfield, Mindoro Island, prior to boarding a C-47D transport. It required about two hours to assemble troops, issue parachutes and other air items, pack their gear, don parachutes and equipment, undergo a safety inspection, and board the aircraft.

Second lift
Detachment, HQ & HQ Company, 503d Parachute Infantry Regiment
2d Battalion, 503d Parachute Infantry Regiment
Detachment, HQ & HQ Battery, 462d Parachute Field Artillery Battalion
Battery B, 462d Parachute Field Artillery Battalion
2d Platoon, Battery D, 162d Parachute Field Artillery Battalion
Company C (less elements), 161st Airborne Engineer Battalion
Service Company (less elements), 503d Parachute Infantry Regiment

Third lift
1st Battalion, 503d Parachute Infantry Regiment
Detachment, HQ & HQ Battery, 462d Parachute Field Artillery Battalion
Battery A, 462d Parachute Field Artillery Battalion
1st Platoon, Battery D, 162d Parachute Field Artillery Battalion

13 Untrained volunteers making a combat jump were authorized jump wings, but in order to remain on jump status they would have to undertake the Parachute Course.

Over Corregidor a C-47 was required to make three passes to drop its stick, with five to six men going out in each pass. The trees and other obstacle hazards of the two tiny DZs are demonstrated here. In the foreground is the empty swimming pool.

were recovered by PT boats. The C-47 carrying 3/503d's Demolition Section and other personnel had an engine stall, and lost altitude. The 26 men jumped over Bataan without injury and were delivered to the Rock the next day. The DZs were secured for the second lift, with some obstacles being removed, and prepared to cover the amphibious landing. The 3/34th Infantry (reinforced) embarked aboard 25 LCMs (landing craft, mechanized) of the 592d Engineer Boat and Shore Regiment, departing from Miriveles Naval Section Base on Bataan's south end. After rounding Corregidor to the west they ran in from the south, hitting Beach Black at 1028 hours. They did not receive heavy fire until the fifth wave arrived. They lost an M4 tank, 105mm M7 self-propelled gun, and a 37mm antitank gun and its jeep to beach mines. Two companies gained a foothold on Malinta Hill. The Japanese had thought the transports were more bombers and then, preoccupied by the paratroopers, were blindsided by the amphibious assault. One group of jumpers blown over the cliff landed near a Japanese observation post. They immediately attacked, killing the Japanese island commander. With their commander dead and phone lines cut the scattered Japanese elements fought in isolated pockets. PT boats and LCMs provided machine-gun fire support, recovered paratroopers, and interdicted Japanese swimmers.

Some officers called for the second lift to be canceled because of casualties and those missing the DZs. Two misdropped .50-cal. machine guns were set up by the Japanese and fired on the second lift. All transports returned to Mindoro by 1000 hours and the second lift departed to arrive in 51 C-47s at 1240 hours, 25 minutes late. Its casualties were not as high as those of the first lift and fewer jumpers missed the DZs.

The 2/503d took over DZ security and mopping up operations while 3/305d continued to clear Topside. It was decided there was no need to drop the 1st Battalion, owing to lighter than expected resistance. Another consideration was that conditions on the DZs meant more jump casualties were inevitable. The third lift was canceled the night of the 16th, although the battalion did not receive word until it was "chuting up." The battalion

A second-lift C-47 unloads jumpers over DZ A, the Corregidor parade ground. The destroyed officers' quarters, craters, gun positions, trees, other obstacles, and the 450ft cliff made this one of the most dangerous DZs ever used.

over-flew the island in the morning, dropping its heavy equipment and ammunition so it would not have to be carried from Bottomside to Topside. The equipment was secured by 2/503d. 1/503d landed at San Marcelino Airfield and was delivered to Beach Black in the afternoon of the 17th.

The 2,022 jumpers of both lifts suffered 13.7 percent jump casualties, lower than expected: 210 were injured on landing, 50 were wounded by ground fire, three died owing to parachute malfunctions, two struck buildings, and 15 were killed by fire in the air or hung in trees. The Navy rescued 16 paratroopers blown into the bay. Initial ground casualties also proved lower than anticipated. Starting on the afternoon of the 17th, 12 C-47s made twice-daily resupply drops from 100ft. A crude L-5 strip was cleared on Topside for medical evacuation.

The pattern of parachute canopies in the foreground lie on DZ A, the parade ground; the "Mile Long Barracks" are to the left. The further pattern of parachutes is DZ B, the golf course. Beyond that can be seen Beach Black and Bottomside, overlooked by Malinta Hill, with 3/34th Infantry landing in LCMs. The island's tail stretches into the distance.

With 3/34th Infantry containing the Japanese inside Malinta Hill, Topside, Middleside, and Bottomside were cleared. Many areas had to be "re-cleared." Because of the rugged terrain it turned into a small-unit fight destroying the defenders in caves, pillboxes, gun positions, buildings, and tunnels and fighting off suicide attacks. 75mm pack howitzers were used for pointblank direct fire into enemy positions. Later, when Topside was secure, the artillery concentrated there and ranged the entire island. The Japanese detonated huge ammunition stocks in tunnels, killing large numbers of themselves and Americans on the surface. On February 24 1/503d and 3/503d attacked to clear the tail while 2/503d mopped up Topside and 3/34th held Bottomside and Malinta Hill. On the 25th 3/34th was withdrawn as its parent 24th InfDiv was preparing for operations in the southern Philippines. It was relieved by 2/151st Infantry under Maj Paul R. Lemasters and Company B, 113th Engineer Combat Battalion from the 38th InfDiv. The surviving defenders retreated down the tail and on the 26th executed a banzai charge, and detonated a massive underground explosion, killing 54 Americans, wounding 145, and blowing a Sherman tank 50 yards. Regardless, at 1600 hours the paratroopers reached the island's tail end. The Rock was not declared secure until March 2 though. That day, MacArthur visited the fortress he had left almost three years previously. Total Rock Force casualties were 1,005 KIA, WIA, and MIA. The 503d PRCT lost 163 KIA, 285 WIA, 7 MIA, and 221 jump and non-combat injuries. Over 5,000 Japanese were killed and 20 prisoners taken with another 200 killed swimming for Bataan.

The 503d departed the Rock aboard LCIs bound for Mindoro on March 8 and 2/151st Infantry remained as the garrison. This was to be the regiment's last combat jump, but not its last operation. MacArthur stated in the unit's Presidential Unit Citation: "Their magnificent courage, tenacity, and gallantry, avenged the victims of Corregidor of 1942, and achieved a significant victory for the United States Army."

The Los Baños raid

Los Baños Internment Camp was 2½ miles southeast of the village by the same name, itself on the southwest shore of Laguna de Bay. The camp contained 2,147 starving American and Allied men, women, and children, held there for over three years. They were guarded by 250 Japanese with several hundred more scattered in the surrounding area. Another 8,000–10,000 troops were within a couple of hours of the camp. It was deemed necessary to rescue the prisoners, as it was feared the Japanese would murder or move them after the fall of Manila.

The 11th AbnDiv was tasked with the mission on February 3, 1945, but was not then able to commence the operation. The division had just reached

Paratroopers set alight the Los Baños Internment Camp barracks to force the liberated internees to board amphibian tractors and evacuate the camp on February 23, 1945. The raid and subsequent liberation of the captives was a masterful operation.

Tagaytay Ridge and the 511th was jumping in. The division still had a long and hard fight before it to penetrate the Genko Line. Los Baños was 20 miles to the east of where the division was now fighting and over 30 miles south of where they would fight through the Genko Line. Nonetheless, the division staff, even while preoccupied with a brutal fight, collected intelligence and undertook tentative planning. By the 15th a picture was developed from aerial photos and information supplied by guerrillas. The target date was set for February 23, a moonless night. On the 20th, Company B, 511th PIR was disengaged and moved to Nichols Field where nine C-47s of the 65th TC Squadron, 433d TC Group landed. The 672d Amphibian Tractor Battalion, under Lt Col Joseph W. Gibbs, with 54 landing vehicles, tracked (LVT[4] amtracs) arrived after driving through Manila from the north. In the meantime the 32-man Provisional Reconnaissance Platoon and 80 guerrillas[14] paddled across Laguna de Bay in canoes on the night of the 21st, moved five miles overland, and were in position on the morning of the 23rd. Their mission was to mark the DZ and amtrac landing beach at 0700 hours, and silently kill outpost sentries.

B/511th under 1st Lt John Ringler was briefed on the mission, parachutes were delivered from Leyte, and the company spent the night under their planes' wings. The company was selected purely because it had the highest strength in the battalion (93), and was augmented by a 28-man battalion machine-gun platoon and at the last minute by a nine-man engineer squad from Company C, 127th Engineer Battalion (130 paratroopers). They launched before dawn and flew over the camp from the west, dropping on the 1,500 x 3,200ft DZ abutting its northeast side. The Reconnaissance Platoon and guerrillas marked the DZ and landing beach with colored smoke grenades and took out the sentries. Company B jumped from 500ft, assembled rapidly with all landing on the DZ without injury, and attacked the camp within 15 minutes as the Reconnaissance Platoon and guerrillas destroyed pillboxes, set fire to the barracks, and killed most of the guards.

14 More guerrillas joined the Reconnaissance Platoon once ashore. Those supporting the platoon for the camp attack were from the Hunters-ROTC 45th Regiment; so named as many members were former college ROTC and Philippine Military Academy cadets. Those securing the beach were from the Marking Fil-Americans group and those marking the DZ were President Quezon's Own Guerrillas, Chinese 48th Squadron, and Hukbalhaps. In all some 500 guerrillas participated.

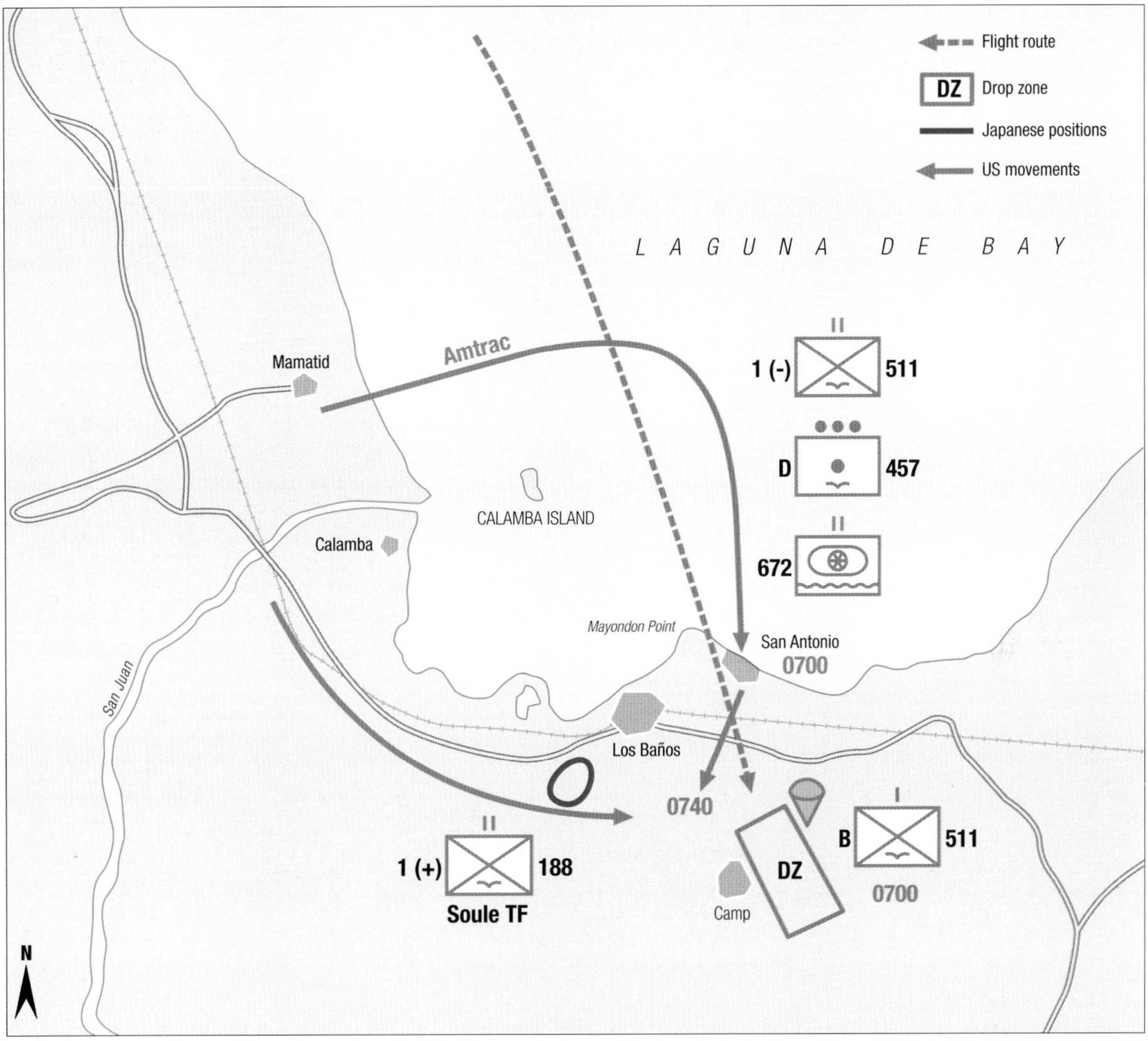
Flight route
DZ Drop zone
Japanese positions
US movements
L A G U N A D E B A Y
Amtrac
Mamatid
1 (-) 511
D 457
672
CALAMBA ISLAND
Calamba
Mayondon Point
San Antonio
0700
San Juan
Los Baños
0740
1 (+) 188
Soule TF
B 511
0700
DZ
Camp
N

The Los Baños Internment Camp operation, February 23, 1945.

The amtracs had an equal challenge as they swam eastward and then swung south at night 7.2 miles across Laguna de Bay from the western shore at Mamatid, a 1 hour 14 minute trip. Amtracs were not designed for lengthy trips and the crews were untrained for night swimming and complex navigation. They landed exactly on schedule near San Antonio north of the camp and west of Los Baños village. Abroad the amtracs were the rest of 1/511th PIR plus a platoon (less elements) of Company C, 127th Engineer Battalion and two 75mm howitzers of Battery D, 457th PFAB. The 472d FAB (105mm) and 675th GFAB were positioned near Calamba to the northwest for fire support and 188th GIR (less 2d Battalion) with Company B, 637th Tank Destroyer Battalion and an engineer bridging unit was moving from that direction for backup (the Soule Task Force). Col Robert H. Soule commanding the 188th GIR was the overall operation commander, but radio contact was never made with any element of the Los Baños Task Force, resulting in it operating on its own.

1/511th elements in amtracs split off and secured the main road and flanking positions. The two howitzers dismounted and shelled nearby hills from which small-arms fire was being received. The main group of amtracs rolled up to the secured camp at 0740 hours, but only a few could enter. The major problem was that the internees did not understand they had to evacuate immediately, thinking the area was liberated for good. To force the milling internees out the paratroops set the barracks aflame and all internees were loaded on amtracs with as many as 50 in each. Miraculously no amtracs broke down, but two sank without loss. With the beachhead secure it was decided the internees would be taken there and evacuated over-water. The initial plan called for 1/511th to fight its way west to link up with Soule Task Force, which had reached a point six miles to the west. If the San Antonio beachhead could not be held only the weaker internees would be evacuated by water and the rest would follow the ground force overland. Resistance was light though and all internees and troops were carried to the beachhead. At 1000 hours the amtracs carrying 30–35 personnel shipped 1,500 internees back to the lake's west shore, receiving ineffective fire en route. Trucks and medical personnel met them at Mamatid. The internees were trucked to New Bilibid Prison, where accommodation had been prepared. 1/511th remained at San Antonio with 720 internees and was picked up by returning amtracs at 1300 hours. The Soule Task Force withdrew to its start line 12 miles to the west with only four KIA. The task force was instrumental in distracting enemy forces from Los Baños. The rescue resulted in two paratroopers KIA, four WIA, and one internee slightly wounded. An unfortunate result of the operation was that the Japanese marauded through the area for several days, murdering at least 1,500 Filipinos and Chinese. The commander responsible was later tried and executed.

Along with the Cabanatuan Prison Camp liberation by the 6th Ranger Battalion and Alamo Scouts five days earlier, the Los Baños liberation was among the war's most successful rescue operations.

On February 23, 1945 the division was given the mission to reverse direction and clear southern Luzon. Initial task organization was as follows:

511th Parachute Infantry Regiment
674th Glider Field Artillery Battalion (75mm)
187th Glider Infantry Regiment
675th Glider Field Artillery Battalion (105mm)
188th Glider Infantry Regiment (less 2d Battalion)
457th Parachute Field Artillery Battalion (75mm)
427th Field Artillery Battalion (105mm)
158th Infantry Regimental Combat Team
147th Field Artillery Battalion (105mm)
2/188th Glider Infantry Regiment
756th Field Artillery Battalion (155mm)
760th Field Artillery Battalion (155mm)

2/188th was responsible for rear security. There was no division reserve. Operations commenced on February 24. No airborne operations were conducted during this phase. 3/511th was attached to 188th GIR in late April and then in early May it became the Division Reserve. The division was down to 7,000 troops and the infantry battalions of course had suffered the highest losses. Even with the 158th RCT attached, itself understrength, the 11th was about two-thirds the strength of an infantry division facing 10,000–17,000 Japanese. Fighting was hard and the division's strength dwindled. The 1st CavDiv was committed in late March, but had to depart in mid April, although it left a regiment attached to the 11th. From March 17 to April 12 the 511th was in Sixth Army Reserve. 11th AbnDiv operations in the south were completed with the fall of Mount Macolod on May 3.

11th Airborne Division attachments on Luzon	
158th Regimental Combat Team (Separate)	3–24 March
147th Field Artillery Battalion (105mm Howitzer)	
59th Engineer Combat Company	
8th Cavalry Regiment, 1st CavDiv[1]	20–30 April
2d Squadron, 7th Cavalry Regiment	
61st Field Artillery Battalion (105mm Howitzer)	
1st & 3d Battalions, 19th Infantry Regiment, 24th InfDiv	5–24 February
2d Battalion, 19th Infantry Regiment, 24th InfDiv	14–24 February
472d Field Artillery Battalion (105mm Howitzer)[2]	21 February–20 July
756th Field Artillery Battalion (155mm Howitzer)	18 March–3 May
760th Field Artillery Battalion (155mm Howitzer)	2 March–10 May
Company A, 44th Tank Battalion [M4]	17 February–3 May
Company B, 85th Chemical Mortar Battalion [4.2in.]	7 April–3 May
Company C, 85th Chemical Mortar Battalion [4.2in.]	27 March–7 April
Company B, 637th Tank Destroyer Battalion [M18]	17 February–3 May
Company C, Boat Battalion, 532d Engineer Boat & Shore Regiment	February
Battery D, 102d AAA Automatic Weapons Battalion [40mm/.50-cal.]	entire period
Cannon Company, 21st Infantry Regiment, 24th InfDiv [M7]	entire period
3498th Ordnance Medium Maintenance Company	10 March–May
5th & 7th Medical Portable Surgical Hospitals	entire period
407th Medical Collecting Company	1 February–10 March
1st Platoon, 605th Medical Clearing Company	1 February–10 March

Notes
1 Dismounted cavalry regiment fighting as infantry, comprising two small battalion-sized squadrons.
2 Redesignated Glider Field Artillery and assigned to 11th AbnDiv on July 20, 1945.

The liberated internees from Los Baños were taken to Mamatid from which they were trucked to New Bilibid Prison for medical care, food, and clothes. Here ¾-ton ambulances transport the weaker internees. Filipino and American flags fly from the prison's towers.

83

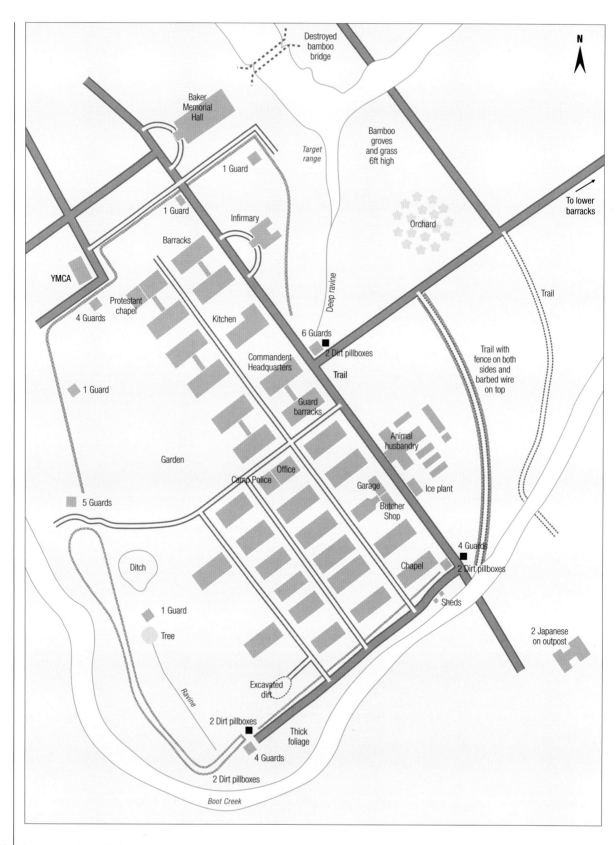

N

Destroyed bamboo bridge

Baker Memorial Hall

Target range

Bamboo groves and grass 6ft high

To lower barracks

1 Guard

1 Guard

Infirmary

Barracks

Orchard

YMCA

Deep ravine

Protestant chapel

4 Guards

Kitchen

Trail

6 Guards

2 Dirt pillboxes

Trail with fence on both sides and barbed wire on top

1 Guard

Commandent Headquarters

Trail

Guard barracks

Animal husbandry

Garden

Office

5 Guards

Camp Police

Garage

Ice plant

Butcher Shop

4 Guards

Ditch

2 Dirt pillboxes

1 Guard

Chapel

Tree

Sheds

2 Japanese on outpost

Ravine

Excavated dirt

2 Dirt pillboxes

Thick foliage

4 Guards

2 Dirt pillboxes

Boot Creek

Internment Camp No.2, Los Baños, Luzon, February 23, 1945.

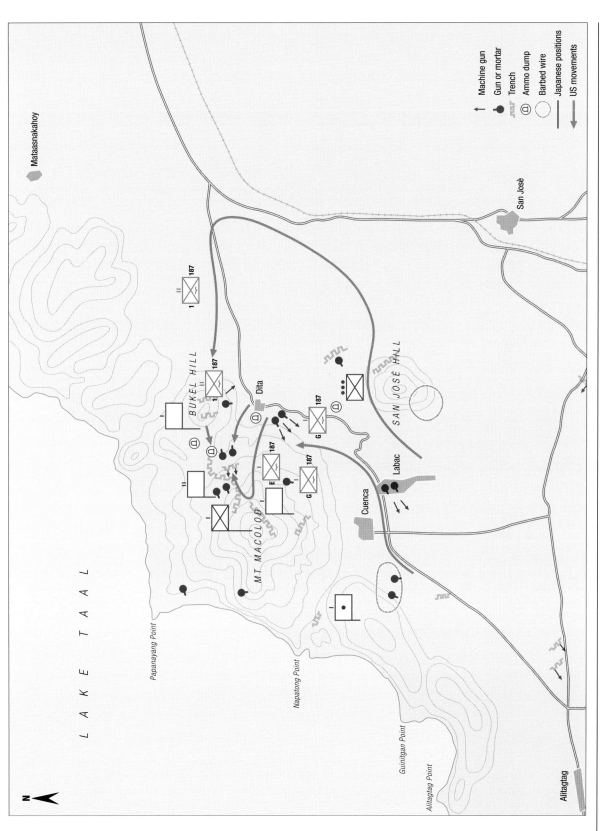

The reduction of Mt Macolod during the clearing of southern Luzon, 187th GIR, March 23–April 20, 1945 – a good example of airborne troops conducting assaults against heavily defended enemy positions.

Fifty-four landing vehicles, tracked, Mk IV (LVT(4)s, or amtracs) of the 672d Amphibian Tractor Battalion carried part of 1/511th PIR across Laguna de Bay to evacuate the Los Baños internees in two lifts. The LVT(4) had a three-man crew and was armed with a .30-cal. M1919A4 and a .50-cal. M2 machine gun.

Between landing on Luzon on February 1 and May 3, the 11th lost 445 KIA, 72 died of wounds (DOW), 3 MIA, 1,307 WIA, and 133 non-combat injured. "The Angels" had killed almost 9,500 Japanese and captured 128. Up to 5,000 guerrillas were attached to the division during the southern operations, and killed almost 2,400 Japanese and captured 35.

The division established a base at Lipa near Lake Taal and south of Los Baños and began to rest and retrain. Over 6,000 replacements arrived in May and parachute and glider training commenced. Ground mock-ups of gliders were used for orientation, as no gliders were available. Mock-ups of C-46s were used to familiarize jumpers arriving in the PTO with the two-door transport, but actual C-46s and gliders soon arrived. The 317th TC Group rotated its four squadrons through training to qualify crews in paratrooper dropping and glider towing.

A major change in the organization of the 11th was made in July 1945 when the December 1944 T/O&E was implemented. Reorganization was accomplished in May and June. This added a third battalion to the 187th GIR; the 188th GIR was converted to parachute on 4 July and authorized a third battalion. The 1st and 2d battalions provided cadres for the new 3d Battalions. Companies were assigned 30–50 percent veterans. Besides replacements the 541st PIR arrived in July and was broken up to fill the expanded 187th, 188th, and 511th. The 764th GFAB was converted to parachute and the 472d FAB, formerly a tractor-drawn 105mm unit, was converted to a 75mm pack howitzer glider battalion and assigned, both on July 20. All other divisional units underwent reorganization with their strength, equipment, and capabilities upgraded. The division's strength increased from 8,596 to 13,035.

The Negros Island operation

The 503d PRCT arrived on Mindoro on March 9, 1945 at its old base. The unit rested, rebuilt, retrained, and absorbed several hundred replacements. Wounded and injured were returned to their former units. However, it was still somewhat understrength. Plans were underway for the reconquest of the central and southern Philippines.

The 40th InfDiv (less elements) had landed on Negros Island southeast of Mindoro and west of Leyte on March 29th (G-Day) and secured part of the island, experiencing little resistance. The 503d on Mindoro had been prepared for parachute reinforcement. The 503d PRCT (less elements) was flown to Panay Island north of Negros on April 8–9 by 317th TC Group and immediately sea-lifted by LCI to Negros, landing at Bacalod on the 9th. 1/503d remained on Mindoro to continue its reorganization and training.

The regiment was soon engaged in the island's mountainous interior. 1/503d arrived by air on April 23 and joined the regiment. They had to be resupplied by air owing to the rugged terrain. Later, Filipino civilians were hired to man-pack supplies. The fighting, climate, and terrain took its toll and by mid May the regiment was reduced to half strength. A few hundred replacements arrived on May 21, but the unit was in poor shape. On June 9 the 503d assumed responsibility for northwestern Negros and the 40th InfDiv was relieved by freshly trained, equipped, and reorganized guerrillas. The 503d was given operational control of 4,000 guerrillas who completed mopping-up operations. The paratroopers conducted rear security until the operation's end on the 20th. Combat losses had been 144 KIA and 370 WIA plus 1,028 men suffering from illness and heat exhaustion, and two murdered by Filipinos. Col Jones rotated back to the States on August 10 and Lt Col Joe S. Lawrie took command.

With the war over in September the regiment was soon broken up, with long-serving troops returned to the States and shorter-serving men reassigned to the 11th AbnDiv. The engineer company was inactivated on Negros on October 25. The skeleton regiment and 462d PFAB arrived at Los Angeles in December 1945. The 503d PIR was inactivated at Camp Anza, CA on the 24th and the 462d on the 21st.

Camalaniugan, Luzon

There was one last combat mission for the 11th AbnDiv on Luzon, and it proved to be the last airborne operation of World War II. In June the Japanese were being pursued in the north and a force was needed to close off an escape route at Aparri near the northeast end of Luzon. The 11th was ordered to dispatch a task force to support the 37th InfDiv.

The target date was to be June 25, 1945, but owing to the speed of the 37th's advance it was moved forward to the 23rd. The 1,010-man Gypsy Task Force was under the command of Lt Col Henry A. Burgess, XO, 511th PIR.

Gypsy Task Force
1st Battalion, 511th Parachute Infantry Regiment
Companies G & I, 3d Battalion, 511th Parachute Infantry Regiment
Battery C, 457th Parachute Field Artillery Battalion
Demolition Platoon, HQ Company, 511th Parachute Infantry Regiment
1st Platoon, Company C, 127th Airborne Engineer Battalion
2d Platoon, 221st Airborne Medical Company
Detachment, Service Company, 511th Parachute Infantry Regiment
Detachments, Special Troops[1]
Note
1 From 11th Parachute Maintenance, 511th Airborne Signal, and 711th Airborne Maintenance Companies.

The task force launched from Lipa Airfield[15] at 0600 hours on the 23rd aboard 54 C-47s, 13 C-46s, a single CG-13A, and six CG-4A gliders. This was the only combat use of US gliders in the PTO and the only combat jump in which C-46s were employed. It seems fitting that the only artillery battery landed by glider in the PTO was a parachute battery. Three hours later they arrived over the DZ, Camalaniugan Airfield[16] between Camalaniugan town three miles to the south and Aparri three miles to the north. A Demolition Platoon pathfinder team had been delivered two days earlier and had marked the DZ with smoke. The pathfinders had linked up with well-trained US Army Forces in the Philippines (Northern Luzon) guerrillas and the DZ was secure. Fighter-bombers laid a smoke screen blinding supposed Japanese gunners in the hills to the southeast. Owing to the 20–25-mph winds, craters, ruts, and flooded paddies two jumpers were killed and 70 injured. Nevertheless, the task force assembled in less than an hour in the kunai grass. The 37th InfDiv's battalion-size Connolly Task Force, which had occupied Aparri, was already

---

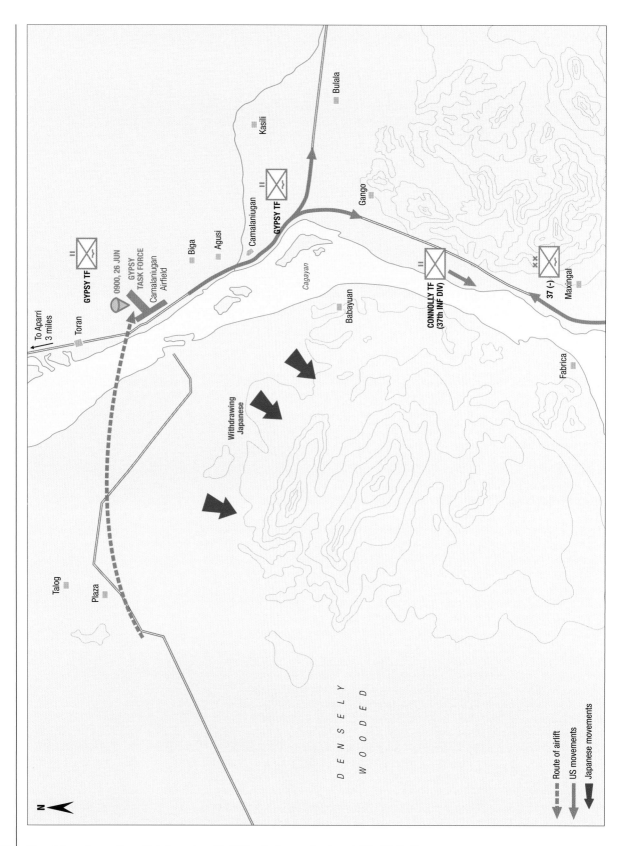

Camaliniugan, Luzon, Gypsy Task Force, June 23, 1945 – the last combat jump in World War II.

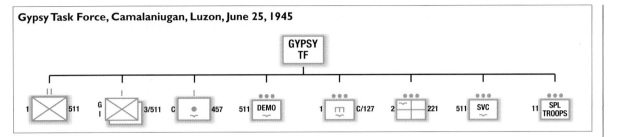

Gypsy Task Force, Camalaniugan, Luzon, June 25, 1945

moving south of Camalaniugan. It would link up with its parent division advancing from the south on the 26th, as did Gypsy Task Force after moving 35 miles south on the same date. Even though Connolly Task Force had secured Camalaniugan the Sixth Army commander ordered the jump in the hope of trapping fleeing enemy troops. There were none to trap; they had already melted into the Sierra Madre in the interior. After searching for Japanese stragglers Gypsy Task Force assembled at Tuguegarao Airfield 55 miles south of Aparri and flew back to Lipa on July 1–2.

Total combat casualties for the 11th AbnDiv on Leyte were 494 KIA, 120 DOW, and 1,926 WIA. Total MIAs are not available, but were few.

On to Japan

The 11th AbnDiv was to have been part of the Sixth Army Reserve for the planned November 1, 1945 invasion of Kyushu, the southernmost of the Home Islands of Japan. Operational plans were never fully developed, but it is possible that tentative DZs and objectives were planned, although the unit was to come ashore by sea or air-landing as a follow-on force. The 503d PRCT was to be on standby for special missions. A deception plan was under development. This included an inland equipment drop behind each of the three corps' beachheads near an airfield, to be dropped the night before the actual landing. The equipment was to appear to be for an airborne unit and it was hoped the Japanese would deploy reserves to cover these "DZs." On the night of the landings more diversionary equipment drops would be made on two airfields further inland. For the projected March 1, 1946 landing on Honshu, Japan's main island, pre-damaged equipment and parachutes would be dropped at various locations. No parachute units were included in the operation's troop list. The 13th AbnDiv and XVIII Abn Corps were scheduled for redeployment to the PTO in late 1945, but they were to be converted to non-airborne.

The 11th AbnDiv was training hard to prepare for Japan. Plans were made for airlifting most personnel, combat equipment, and essential air-transportable vehicles. A rear echelon to be delivered by sealift was planned. Rumors were rampant that the operation would involve a jump, and then that it would not. The first atomic bomb was then dropped, and on August 10 Japan's intent to surrender was announced.

The division celebrated, relieved that it was spared from a long, brutal campaign; however, its work was not finished. At 0530 hours, August 11 the division was alerted for advance elements to be ready to fly out in four hours. Trucks were borrowed from other units to move troops to Lipa, Nicholas, Nielson, and Clark Fields where they loaded aboard 351 C-46s, 151 C-47s, and 99 B-24 bombers[17] of the 54th TC Group. With the Philippines secured sufficient transports were available for once, although some had to make two lifts. It required four days to fly the division to Okinawa, where it was held on standby for airlift to Japan. In all 11,100 troops, 120 jeeps, and 1,161,000 lb. of supplies and equipment were lifted by the 15th. The rear echelon and

---

17 Pressed into emergency service as a transport with jury-rigged seats, the B-24 carried 20 passengers.

A practice jump by the 511th PIR at Dobodura, New Guinea. With the last airborne operations conducted on Luzon, none were foreseen for the coming invasion of the Japanese Home Islands. By no means, though, were the airborne considered obsolete.

vehicles were loaded on ships. The move was not without its cost. A B-24 and C-46 crashed killing 41 division troops, including much of the Reconnaissance Platoon.

The division spent two weeks on Okinawa while plans were made to fly into Atsugi Airbase west of Yokohama and southwest of Tokyo. A backup plan was developed to parachute battalions into a park inside Tokyo. C-47s lacked the range for a round trip between Okinawa and Atsugi and C-46s had an insufficient fuel safety margin. Fuel in Japan could not be assured. B-24 bombers and four-engine C-54 transports would lift the division. The C-54s had been assembled from all over the world by Air Transport Command. The division went combat loaded and did not know what kind of reception the Japanese would provide. The division also trained the follow-on 27th InfDiv for airlift.

The Japanese authorities were ordered to have 400 trucks and 100 sedans ready at Atsugi. Z-Day was August 28 and the division's mission was to secure Atsugi Airbase, evict all Japanese people within three miles, provide security for the advance echelon of MacArthur's GHQ, US Army Pacific, Eighth Army and other headquarters, and occupy Yokohama. A provisional Honor Guard Company was formed with a platoon of men at least 5ft 11in. tall from each regiment and attached to 3/188th PIR. Z-Day was delayed two days owing to a typhoon slowing the Third Fleet. Regardless, on the 28th, an advance party landed at Atsugi to ensure Japanese compliance and assess conditions. It was decided only C-54s would be employed. The first took off at 0100 hours, August 30 and landed at 0600 hours with a steady flow following. The division CP was soon established in Yokohama and 123 C-54s had delivered 4,200 troops. The entire division was in place by September 7 with 11,708 men, 600 jeeps and trailers, and 640 tons of supplies and equipment. The Japanese were completely passive and no difficulties arose. The division occupied the west side of Tokyo Bay south of the capital.

On September 15 the 11th was relieved by the Americal Division and moved to Hokaido Island, setting up headquarters at Sapporo. Most of the division, though, was located on Honshu Island to the south with a rear headquarters in Sendai. The artillery battalions were converted to infantry occupation troops. Soldiers serving overseas for long periods began to be rotated home. Replacements comprised recent draftees and few were parachute qualified. A parachute school was established at Yanome south of Sandai, graduating over 3,300 men. When the 503d PRCT departed the Philippines for the States its short-serving troops were reassigned to the 11th. The jump school was moved to Carolus Field, but was soon closed as virtually the entire division was jump qualified.

Maj Gen Swing relinquished command of the division in January 1948 having commanded it from its inception in February 1943 – a record five years.[18] In 1947/48 the parachute and glider infantry and artillery units were all redesignated "airborne" with both parachute and glider capabilities. Swing's dual concept was finally realized. In May 1949 the division redeployed to Ft. Campbell, KY. The 187th Airborne Infantry Regiment (AIR) became a separate airborne regimental combat team and fought in Korea from 1950 to 1953. To replace it the 503d AIR was reactivated in the 11th. The 11th deployed to West Germany in 1956 and on July 1, 1958 it was inactivated with its assets becoming the 24th InfDiv, which maintained some airborne units. The 11th was briefly reactivated in 1963 as the 11th Air Assault Division (TEST) to develop the helicopter airmobile concept. It was inactivated in 1965 to become the 1st CavDiv (Airmobile), which still contained an airborne artillery and three airborne infantry battalions.

---

18 Brig Gen Frank Dorn served as acting commander from February to June 1946.

Chronology

1940
July 1   Parachute Test Platoon formed at Ft Benning, GA.
October 26   Marine parachute training commences.

1941
February 25   Provisional Parachute Group formed at Ft Benning.
March 21   Provisional Parachute Group redesignated as Airborne Command.

1942
March 2   503d PIR activated at Ft Benning.
July 9   FSSF activated at Ft William Harrison, MT.
August 7   1st Parachute Battalion lands on Gavutu.

1943
January 5   511th PIR activated at Camp Toccoa, GA.
February 25   11th Airborne Division (AbnDiv) activated at Camp Mackall, NC.
April 1   1st Marine Parachute Regiment activated on New Caledonia.
August 12   541st PIR activated at Ft Benning.
August 15   FSSF lands on Kiska Island.
September 5   503d PIR jumps at Nadzab, New Guinea.
October 28   2d Parachute Battalion lands on Choiseul Island.
December 6–11   Knollwood Maneuvers.

1944
February 29   1st Marine Parachute Regiment deactivated.
March 1   Airborne Command redesignated Airborne Center at Camp Mackall, NC.
July 3–4   503d PIR jumps on Noemfoor Island.
October 20   Initial Leyte landing.
December 1   Battery A, 457th Parachute Field Artillery Battalion (PFAB) jumps at Manarawat, Leyte.
December 15   503d Parachute Regimental Combat Team (PRCT) lands on Mindoro.

1945
January 7   Initial Luzon landing.
February 2   11th AbnDiv (less elements) lands on Luzon.
February 3-4   511th PIR jumps on Tagaytay Ridge, Luzon.
February 16   503d PRCT jumps on Corregidor.
February 23   Company B, 511th PIR liberates Los Baños, Luzon.
April 9   503d PRCT lands on Negros Island.
May 7   Germany surrenders.
June 23   1st Battalion, 511th PIR jumps at Camalaniugan, Luzon.
August 6   Atomic bomb dropped on Hiroshima.
August 9   Atomic bomb dropped on Nagasaki.
August 14   Japan announces its intent to surrender unconditionally.
August 20   541st PIR deactivated.
August 28   11th AbnDiv arrives in Japan.
September 2   Japan surrenders.

Bibliography

Arthur, Anthony *Deliverance at Los Baños*. New York: St. Martin's Press, 1985.

Burhans, Robert D. *The First Special Service Force: A War History of the North Americans 1942–1944*. Washington, DC: Infantry Journal Press, 1947.

Christ, James F. *Mission Raise Hell: The U.S. Marines on Choiseul, October–November 1943*. Annapolis, MD: Naval Institute Press, 2006.

Devlin, Gerard M. *Paratrooper! The Saga of the US Army and Marine Parachute and Glider Combat Troops in World War II*. St. Martin's Press, NY: 1979.

Field Manual 31-30, *Tactics and Techniques of Air-Borne Troops, May 20, 1942.*

Flanagain, Edward M, Jr. *The Angels: A History of the 11th Airborne Division, 1943–1946*. Washington, DC: Infantry Journal Press, 1948.

Flanagain, Edward M, Jr. *The Los Baños Raid: The 11th Airborne Division Jumps at Dawn*. Novato, CA: Presidio Press, 1986. (Re-released 1999 as *Angles at Dawn: The Los Baños Raid*.)

Flanagain, Edward M, Jr. *Corregidor: The Rock Assault Force, 1945*. Novato, CA: Presidio Press, 1988.

Flanagain, Edward M, Jr. *The Rakkasans: The Combat History of the 187th Airborne Infantry*. Novato, CA: Presidio Press, 1997.

Guthrie, Bennett M. *Three Winds of Death: The Saga of the 503d Parachute Regimental Combat Team in the South Pacific*. Chicago: Adams Press, 1985.

Hoffman, Jon T. *Silk Chutes and Hard Fighting: US Marine Corps Parachute Units in World War II*. History and Museums Division, HQ, Marine Corps, 1999.

Huston, James A. *Out of the Blue: US Army Airborne Operations in World War II*. West Lafayette, IN: Purdue University Studies, 1972.

Joyce, Kenneth H. *Snow Plough and the Jupiter Deception: The True Story of the 1st Special Service Force*. St. Catharines, Canada: Vanwell Publishing, 2005.

Quarrie, Bruce. *Airborne Assault: Parachute Forces in Action, 1940–91*. Sparford, UK: Patrick Stephens Ltd., 1991.

Ross, Robert T. *Supercomandos: First Special Service Force, 1942–1944, an Illustrated History*. Landcaster, PA: Schiffer Books, 2000.

Rottman, Gordon L. *US Marine Corps Order of Battle: Ground and Air Units in the Pacific War, 1939–1945*. Westport, CT: Greenwood Publishing, 2001.

Rottman, Gordon L. *World War II Pacific Island Guide: A Geo-Military Study*. Westport, CT: Greenwood Publishing, 2001.

Smith, Michael S. *Bloody Ridge: The Battle that Saved Guadalcanal*. New York: Pocket Books, 2000.

Smith, Robert R. *US Army in World War II: Triumph in the Philippines*. Washington, DC: Center for Military History, 1963.

Stanton, Shelby L. *World War II Order of Battle. An Encyclopedic Reference to US Army Ground Forces from Battalion through Division 1939–46*. Mechanicsburg, PA: Stackpole Books, 2006.

Updegraph, Charles L., Jr. *US Marine Corps Special Units of World War II*. Washington, DC: History and Museums Division, HQ, Marine Corps, 1972.

Weeks, John *The Airborne Soldier*. Poole, UK: Blandford Press, 1982.

Glossary and abbreviations

AA	antiaircraft	LMG	light machine gun
AbnDiv	Airborne Division	LST	landing ship, tank
AIR	Airborne Infantry Regiment	LVT	landing vehicle, tracked ("amtrac")
amtrac	amphibian tractor (see LVT)	MarDiv	Marine Division
AT	antitank	MIA	missing in action
BAR	Browning automatic rifle	NCO	non-commissioned officer
CO	Commanding Officer	PFAB	Parachute Field Artillery Battalion
CP	command post	PIB	Parachute Infantry Battalion
DOW	died of wounds	PIR	Parachute Infantry Regiment
DZ	drop zone	PRCT	Parachute Regimental Combat Team
FAB	Field Artillery Battalion	PTO	Pacific Theater of Operations
FMF	Fleet Marine Force	RCT	Regimental Combat Team
FSSF	First Special Service Force	SMG	submachine gun
GFAB	Glider Field Artillery Battalion	SNLF	Special Naval Landing Force (Japanese)
GIR	Glider Infantry Regiment	TC	troop carrier
HE	high explosive	T/O	Table of Organization
HMG	heavy machine gun	T/O&E	Table of Organization and Equipment
HQ	headquarters	USAAF	United States Army Air Forces
IIIAC	III Amphibious Corps	USMC	United States Marine Corps
IMAC	I Marine Amphibious Corps	WIA	wounded in action
InfDiv	Infantry Division (US Army)	WO	warrant officer
KIA	killed in action	WP	white phosphorus
LCI	landing craft, infantry	XO	Executive Officer (second-in-command)
LCM	landing craft, mechanized		
LCP(R)	landing craft, personnel (ramp)		

Army and Marine Corps officer ranks

2d Lt	2d Lieutenant
1st Lt	1st Lieutenant
Capt	Captain
Maj	Major
Lt Col	Lieutenant Colonel
Col	Colonel
Brig Gen	Brigadier General ("one-star")
Maj Gen	Major General ("two-star")

Index